Men-at-Arms • 554

Czechoslovak Armies 1939–45

Nigel Thomas PhD • Illustrated by Johnny Shumate

Series editors Martin Windrow & Nick Reynolds

OSPREY PUBLISHING
Bloomsbury Publishing Plc
Kemp House, Chawley Park, Cumnor Hill, Oxford OX2 9PH, UK
29 Earlsfort Terrace, Dublin 2, Ireland
1385 Broadway, 5th Floor, New York, NY 10018, USA
E-mail: info@ospreypublishing.com
www.ospreypublishing.com

OSPREY is a trademark of Osprey Publishing Ltd

First published in Great Britain in 2024

© Osprey Publishing Ltd, 2024

A catalogue record for this book is available from the British Library

ISBN: PB: 9781472856852; eBook: 9781472856845; ePDF: 9781472856838;
XML: 9781472856869

24 25 26 27 28 10 9 8 7 6 5 4 3 2 1

Editor: Martin Windrow
Index by Fionbar Lyons
Typeset by PDQ Digital Media Solutions, Bungay, UK
Printed in India by Replika Press Private Ltd

Osprey Publishing supports the Woodland Trust, the UK's leading woodland conservation charity.

To find out more about our authors and books, visit
www.ospreypublishing.com. Here you will find extracts, author interviews, details of forthcoming events, and the option to sign up for our newsletter.

Acknowledgements

Nigel Thomas would like to thank the following correspondents for their interest, generosity, patience and kindness in the preparation of this book: Jan Vogeltanz PhD, Miroslav Hus PhD, and Christopher Harrod. He must also acknowledge the printed work of Jan Vogeltanz PhD, Miroslav Hus PhD, Milan Polak, and Robert Speychal.

He would also like to thank his wife Heather and sons Alexander and Dominick for their tireless encouragement and support.

For further information on Nigel Thomas or to contact him, please refer to his website: nt-associates.com

TITLE PAGE
Troops of the Red Army's '1st Czechoslovak Army Corps in the USSR' marching through a town in eastern Czechoslovakia early in 1945. They display Bohemian Lion and Shield cap badges, and wear M1930 Czechoslovak greatcoats along with some Red Army items, such as fleece winter caps and a field cape. Some are armed with 7.62mm Soviet PPSh-41 sub-machine guns. (Nigel Thomas Collection)

Abbreviations used in this text

AA	anti-aircraft	Grp	group	PTN	platoon
Armd	armoured	Indep	independent	PU	Czech resistance organization
Arty	artillery	KONR	Russian Liberation Army (*also* ROA)	PWZ	Czech resistance organization
AT	anti-tank	KVV	Czech Army District	Regt	regiment
Bde	brigade	Lt	lieutenant, or light	ROA	Russian Liberation Army (*also* KONR)
Bn	battalion	LtCol	lieutenant-colonel	2iC	second-in-command
Bty/s	battery/ies	LtGen	lieutenant-general	SF	Sudeten Free Corps
Capt	captain	Maj	major	Sigs	Signals (branch of service)
Cav	cavalry	MajGen	major-general	SMG	sub-machine gun
Coy/s	company/ies	MG	machine gun	SOE	Special Operations Executive (British)
Cpl	corporal	MT	motor transport	SOS	State Defence Guard
Div	division	Mtn	mountain	SVC	Shanghai Volunteer Corps
Drgn	dragoon	Med	medical	Tspt	transport
Eng	engineers	MNO	Czech Ministry of Defence	UVOD	Czech resistance coordination
FS	Sudeten Volunteer Service	Mot	motorized	WO	warrant officer
Gen	general	NCO	non-commissioned officer	ZVV	Czechoslovak Army Region
GHQ	general headquarters	ON	Czech resistance organization		
GOC	general officer commanding	PRNV	Czech resistance coordination		

CZECHOSLOVAK ARMIES 1939–45

INTRODUCTION

Czechoslovakia as an independent Western Slav state dates from the Kingdom of Bohemia, established in 1198 but absorbed in 1526 by the Austrian (1867, Austro–Hungarian) Empire. From the 1770s onwards, Czech national consciousness became increasingly influential, both at home and later among emigrant communities.

At the outbreak of World War I in August 1914, leading Czech émigré politicians such as Tomáš Garrigue Masaryk (1850–1937) declared allegiance to the Entente (the Allies – principally France, Great Britain and Russia) against the Central Powers (principally Austro–Hungary and Germany). About 150,000 Czechoslovaks and members of the Czechoslovak diaspora served in the French, Italian and Russian forces during the Great War, survivors being united in 1918 as the Czechoslovak Legion.[1] On 28 October 1918, Masaryk, designated 'president-protector', proclaimed Czechoslovakia's independence, and served as its first president from 14 November.

Between the wars, Czechoslovakia prospered economically, developing a strong industrial base and a well-equipped army. However, it suffered the disadvantage of having a disunited multicultural population, though dominated by the Czechs. According to the 1921 census, Czechoslovakia had an area of 54,400 square miles and a population of 13,410,750, with ethnic groups dispersed across five administrative provinces. The most numerous groups were the 9,362,287 Czechs in Bohemia, Moravia and Silesia, and the 3,061,369 German-speaking Austrians (known as 'Sudeten Germans', after the Sudeten Mountains). The latter were numerous in four Bohemian and Moravian border regions: German Bohemia (formed 29 October 1918), Sudetenland (30 October 1918), Bohemian Forest Region, and German Southern Moravia (both 3 November 1918). These Sudeten regions hoped to unite and join the new German Republic, but they were promptly abolished by the Czechoslovak government in December 1918. In 1921, there were also 2,898,361 Slovaks in Slovakia, 592,044 Rusyns in Subcarpathian Ruthenia, and 218,000 Jews, 59,383 Poles and 19,932 Hungarians distributed across Czechoslovakia.

Czechoslovak Armed Forces, October 1918–March 1920

The Czechoslovak Home Army (*Československá domácí vojska*) was formed on 28 October 1918 with Czechs and Slovaks from the Austro–Hungarian Army, joined by legionary veterans of the French, Italian and Russian armies, to form the Czechoslovak Armed Forces (*Československá branná*

General (*Armádní generál*) Jan Syrový, wearing ceremonial khaki M1930 uniform. Arguably the most important Czechoslovak soldier of the 20th century, he lost his right eye during World War I serving with the Czechoslovak Legion on the Eastern Front. During the 1920s–30s, he served successively as Army Chief of Staff, Army Inspector-General, Defence Minister and Prime Minister. Syrový signed the Munich Agreement on 30 Sept 1938, was appointed President (5 Oct–1 Dec 1938), and resigned as Defence Minister on 27 Apr 1939. For uniform details, see commentary to Plate A1. (Photographer unknown; Wikimedia Commons/Public domain)

---

1   For more detail on this complex process, see MAA 447 *The Czech Legion 1914–20.*

A troop of Czechoslovak mounted Dragoons on parade, 1936. They wear M1932/34 helmets and M1930 field uniforms, but with scarlet service-dress riding breeches (compare with Plate F3). They hold M1924 cavalry sabres, and have either M1923 (ČZ Vz.23) short rifles or M1933 (Vz.33) carbines slung across their backs. The Czechoslovak Army was principally a mechanized force, and on 1 Jan 1936 the mounted cavalry were reduced to 13 regiments for field reconnaissance. (Nigel Thomas Collection)

moc). Popularly abbreviated to Czechoslovak Army *(Československá armáda),* this was subordinate to the Ministry of National Defence *(Ministerstvo národní obrany* – MNO).

Czechoslovakia fought three successful border wars to secure its national territory: firstly against the Austrian/German border regions (October–December 1918); secondly, to secure the Czech–Polish Cieszyn district (23 January–3 February 1919); and finally, against communist Hungary in the Hungarian–Czechoslovak War (April–June 1919) over Slovakia and Subcarpathian Ruthenia. Meanwhile, the units of the Czechoslovak Legion still in Russia fought the Bolsheviks in Siberia (25 May 1918–1 March 1920), before the last legionaries were shipped home in September 1920.

On 1 January 1920, the Czechoslovak Army was reorganized into 12 (infantry) divisions numbered 1–12, each with two infantry brigades (1–24) plus supporting units and services. Within two months, 19 more brigades were added: 1st & 2nd Inf, 12th Mountain, 1st–3rd Cavalry and 1st–12th Artillery, 1st & 2nd Heavy and 25th Light Artillery.

The 'Little Entente', 1921–38

On the initiative of Edvard Beneš, the Czechoslovak foreign minister, and with French support, this pact was concluded between April 1921 and April 1922 by Czechoslovakia, France, Romania, and the Kingdom of Serbs, Croats and Slovenes (from October 1929, Yugoslavia). It was essentially a military alliance against Hungary, which was bitterly resentful of the forfeiture of territory it had suffered after the Great War. The Little Entente prevented the Austrian Emperor, Karl I, from reclaiming his Hungarian throne in March 1921; but it was later intimidated by Nazi Germany, and in April 1937 Romania and Yugoslavia refused to aid Czechoslovakia against Hitler. This fatally compromised the alliance, which was disbanded in September 1938 following the German occupation of Sudetenland. (On 16 May 1935, the Soviet Union had also concluded a mutual assistance pact with Czechoslovakia, but Stalin failed to honour it when Germany annexed Sudetenland.)

PRELUDE, 1933–38

Emboldened by Hitler's rise to power in Germany on 30 January 1933, Konrad Henlein, the Sudeten German leader, formed the Sudeten German Home Front (*Sudetendeutsche Heimatfront* – SDH) on 19 April 1935. Redesignated the Sudeten German Party (*Sudetendeutsche Partei* – SdP), this numbered over 1.3 million members in June 1938.

Meanwhile, during 1935–38, the Czechoslovak Army built a network of concrete border fortifications, inspired by the French Maginot Line, on Czechoslovakia's borders with Germany, Hungary and Poland. On 23 October 1936, the Czechoslovak Customs Border Guard (*Finanční stráž* – FS), urban State Police (*Státní policie*), Rural Police (*Četnictvo*), and military reservists were formed into the 30,000-strong State Defence Guard (*Stráž Obrany Státu* – SOS), commanded by Army officers and comprising 31 named border battalions: Bratislava, Bruntál, České Budějovice, Chust, Domažlice, Falknov nad Ohří, Hodonín, Jindřichův Hradec, Jičín, Kadaň, Košice, Levice, Liptovský Mikuláš, Liberec, Litoměřice, Lučenec, Michalovce, Moravská Ostrava, Moravské Budějovice, Most, Nové Zámky, Praha (Prague), Rimavská Sobota, Rychnov nad Kněžnou, Spisska Nová Ves, Strakonice, Stríbno, Šumperk, Užhorod, Žilina and Znojmo. The following 7 Bns were planned but not formally established: Brno, Hranice, Kroměříž, Pardubice, Plzeň (Pilsen), Poděbrady, and Tábor.

CZECHOSLOVAK ARMY ORGANIZATION, 10 SEPTEMBER 1930–30 SEPTEMBER 1938
Arms and services
Units were divided between Combat Arms – Infantry, Mobile Forces, Artillery, Engineers and Air Corps; and Services – Legal, Medical, Chaplains, Veterinary, etc. The service branches comprised soldiers with technical qualifications not held by combat personnel, and were equivalent to Austro–Hungarian and Imperial German Army military 'officials'. Space prevents more than the briefest mentions of these services here.

Higher formations
Czechoslovak Army formations and units were divided between four Army Districts (*Zemské vojenské velitelství* – ZVV): Bohemia (HQ Prague); Moravia (Brno); West Slovakia (Bratislava); and East Slovakia & Sub-Carpathian Rus/Ruthenía (Košice). Upon the general mobilization of 30 September 1938, they formed four Armies numbered I–IV, and a GHQ Reserve (*Hlavní velitelství* – HV). An Army (*Armáda*) comprised 1 or 2 Corps, an Army Reserve of at least divisional strength, and various sub-divisional units. Seven Corps numbered I–VII were formed on 15 October 1935, joined on 30 September 1938 by VIII Corps. A Corps (*sbor*) comprised 1–2 Divisions (or equivalent), plus border units. Four temporary divisional groupings (1st–4th Groups – sing: *skupina*) were formed in May 1938 with infantry, border and artillery units.

Six of the Corps (I–IV, VI & VII) contained six Border Regions (numbered XI–XVI). Each Region (*Hrahiční pásmo*) contained 1–3

Emanuel Moravec was a career Army officer disillusioned by the 1938 Munich Agreement, but when the Bohemia–Moravia Protectorate was proclaimed on 16 Mar 1939, he embraced Nazi ideology. As Minister of Education, he also headed the paramilitary *Kuratorium* modelled on the Hitler Youth. Regarded as the most important Czechoslovak collaborator, Moravec committed suicide in May 1945.

This photo shows him as a colonel (*plukovník*) of the General Staff in 1938, wearing M1930 khaki service dress. Note on the cap the crossed combat-arms swords on the diamond-shaped gilt badge, the single thick gold plaited chin-cord worn by both field-grade and subaltern officers, and the 4 rank stars displayed on either side of the band, repeating those on his shoulder straps.

Emanuel Moravec was not related to František Moravec, wartime chief of Czechoslovak Military Intelligence in London; the latter had in fact considered assassinating Emanuel Moravec instead of Reinhard Heydrich. (Vladimir Prochazka/Wikimedia Commons/Public domain)

Table 1: Battle Order of Czechoslovak Army, 30 Sept 1938

GHQ Reserve: 4 Inf Div 'Heyduk' (54, 71, 80 Inf Regts, 4 Lt Arty Regt,Tank Coy); **12 Inf Div 'Fajnor'** (70, 86, 95 Inf Regts, 12 Lt Arty Regt); **13 Inf Div 'Úprka'** (72, 97, 98 Inf Regts, 13 Lt Arty Regt); **16 Inf Div 'Jablonsky'** (1, 2 Mtn Inf Regts, 41 Inf Regt, 16 Lt Arty Regt); **22 Inf Div 'Hviezdoslav'** (7 Mtn Inf Regt, 66, 87 Inf Regts, 204 Lt Arty Regt); **1 Mobile Div 'Kazimír':** 1 Cav Bde (1, 5 Drgn Regts, 4 Cycle Bn, 81 Lt Arty Bn), 1 Mot Bde (2, 3 Tank Regts, 1, 2 Mot Train Bns, 84 Lt Arty Bn); 1 Recce Bn; 81, 85 AA Coys; 83, 84 AT Coys.

VIII Corps 'Tajovsky': 9 Inf Div 'Hodža' (62, 73, 89 Inf Regts, 9 Lt Arty Regt); **15 Inf Div 'Jánošík'** (9, 17, 33 Inf Regts, 15 Lt Arty Regt, Tank Coy); **21 Inf Div 'Šafarík'** (91 Inf Regt, 5, 6 Mtn Inf Regts, 203 Lt Arty Regt).

I. Armáda 'Havlíček'. Army Reserve: 18 Inf Div 'Erbe' (55, 78, 88 Inf Regts, 18 Lt Arty Regt, Tank Coy).

I Corps 'Smetana': 1 Inf Div (5, 28, 38 Inf Regts, 1 Arty Regt); **2 Inf Div 'Mácha'** (68, 85, 96 Inf Regts, 2 Lt Arty Regt, Tank Coy); **5 Inf Div 'Bezruč'** (51, 61, 79 Inf Regts, 5 Lt Arty Regt, Tank Coy); **1 Group 'Vlastimil'** (42, 46 Inf Regts; 1, 5 Mtn Inf Regts; 1, 18 Arty Regts); **4 Group 'Vlk'; Border Region XI 'Dalibor'** (Border District 32 'Milulás').

II Corps 'Dvorák': 3 Inf Div 'Holeček' (3 Mtn Inf Regt, Tank Coy, Border District 33 'Dominik' (52, 92, 94 Inf Regts, 13 Lt Arty Regt, Tank Coy); **17 Inf Div 'Blodek'** (16, 27 Inf Regts, 3 Mtn Inf Regt, 17 Lt Arty Regt); **Border Region XII 'Otakar'** (Border Districts 33 'Dominik', 34 'Borivoj', 35 'Vítežslav').

II. Armáda 'Jirašek'. Army Reserve: 8 Inf Div 'Manès' (58, 65, 90 Inf Regts, 8 Lt Arty Regt).

IV Corps 'Myselbek': 7 Inf Div 'Aleš' (56, 63, 84 Inf Regts, 7 Lt Arty Regt); **Border Region XIII 'Rostislav'** (Border Districts 37 'Florián', 36 'Prokop').

III Armáda 'Štefánik'. Army Reserve: 10 Inf Div 'Tomašik' (57, 75, 76 Inf Regts, 10 Lt Arty Regt); **11 Inf Div 'Dobrovsky'** (64, 82 Inf Regts, 8 Mtn Inf Regt, 11 Lt Arty Regt; **3 Mobile Div 'David':** 3 Cav Bde (3, 11 Drgn Regts, 3 Cycle Bn, 83 Lt Arty Bn), 3 Motorized Bde (5 Tank Bn, 87 Lt Arty Bn, 3 Mot Train Bn); 1 Recce Bn; 83, 87 AA Coys; 87, 88 AT Coys; **2 Group 'Jaromir'** (31, 38 Inf Regts, 3 Mtn Bn, 1, 19, 51, 102 Arty Regts).

VII Corps 'Hurban': Border District 39 'Rafael'; Border District 36 'Prokop'; **Border Region XIII** (Border District 37 'Florián'); **Border Region XV 'Adam'** (Border District 40 'Medard'); **Border Region XVI 'Ferdinand'** (Border Districts 41 'Alfons', 42 'Karol').

IV. Armáda 'Neruda'.

III Corps 'Halek': 14 Inf Div 'Fibich' (3, 27, 43 Inf Regts, 14 Mot Inf Regt, 14 Lt Arty Regt); **19 Inf Div 'Arbes'** (60, 74, 81 Inf Regts, 19 Lt Arty Regt); **Border Region XIV 'Svatopluk'** (Border District 38 'Cyril'); **2 Mobile Div 'Ondrej':** 2 Cav Bde (2, 6 Drgn Regts, 2 Cycle Bn, 82 Lt Arty Bn), 2 Mot Bde (10, 30 Mot Inf Bns, 86 Mot Arty Bn, 2 Mot Train Bn, 82, 86 AA Coys; 85, 86 AT Coy.

V Corps 'Kolár': 6 Inf Div 'Kalvoda' (53, 77, 93 Inf Regts, 6 Lt Arty Regt); **20 Inf Div 'Bernolák'** (59, 67, 83 Inf Regts, 20 Lt Arty Regt).

VI Corps 'Rázus': Border District 31 'Blažej'; **4 Mobile Div 'Vojtech':** 4 Cav Bde (4, 8 Drgn Regts, 1 Cycle Bn, 84 Lt Arty Bn), 4 Mot Bde (4, 7, 8 Tank Bns); 4, 24 Mot Mtn Bns, 85 Mot Arty Bn, 4 Mot Train Bn, 84, 88 Lt Arty Coys; 89, 90 AA Coys; 83, 84 AT Coys.

Border Districts (sing: *Hrahični oblast).* There were 12 Districts (numbered 31–42), controlling the extensive frontier fortifications built in 1935–38.

Combat arms:
Infantry

Castle Guards Unit *(Hradní stráž).* Formed 6 Dec 1918 to guard the president in Prague Castle, and other important buildings. It was reformed 1 June 1929 with three coys, commemorating the Czechoslovak Legion's French, Italian and Russian units in the Great War.

Infantry Divisions. Twelve Divisions (numbered 1–12) were formed on 1 Jan 1920. On 15 Oct 1937, three Inf Divs (numbered 13–15) were formed, followed on 1 Jan 1938 by 16–17 Inf Divs. On 1 Jan 1938, all 17 divs were designated 'Inf Divs', and on 30 Sept 1938 the mobilized army expanded to 22 Inf Divs (numbered 1–22). There were also *Skupina 1* and *2*, divisional-sized formations but with minimal HQ units.

An Infantry Div *(Pěši Divise)* comprised HQ units; three Inf Regts (sing: *Pluk*), each with three Battalions (I–III). A Bn *(Prapor)* was divided into 3 companies, a Coy (*Rota*) into 4 Platoons, a Ptn (sing: *Četa*) into sections (sing: *Družstvo*). There were also three Light Artillery Regts (*oddíl*, with horse and motorized arty bns); a Mixed Support Bn including cyclists and horse cavalry, and a light tank platoon. During 1928–37, a total of 48 Line Inf Regts were formed (numbered 1–48), grouped sequentially in pairs and allocated to 1–24 Inf Bdes, which in turn were allocated to 12 Inf Divisions.

Mountain Infantry (*Horská pechota*). Four Mtn Inf Regts (each with bns numbered I–IV) were formed in the Slovakian Tatra mountain region on 15 Jan 1920, and reorganized on 1 Apr into 1st & 2nd Mtn Inf Bdes and a Mtn Arty Regiment. On 1 Jan 1921, the regts were reorganized into 12 independent Mtn Inf Bns, numbered sequentially 1–12. On 1 Jan 1938, 1st & 2nd Bdes were subordinated to the 6th & 7th Inf Divs respectively.

Border Infantry (*Hraničaská pechota*). Ten Border Inf Bns (numbered 1–10) were formed on 15 Jan 1920, with 11th Bn added on 15 Sept 1933, and 50th Bn on 17 July 1938. Later, seven of these bns were expanded into Regts: 3 (15 Sept 1938); 4 (15 Aug 1937); 6 (1 Jan 1938); 11 (15 Sept 1938); 17 & 18 (1 Aug 1938); and 19 (1 Jan 1938).

Bicycle Infantry units (*Cyklistické jednotky*). Three company-equivalent bicycle squadrons (numbered 1–3) were formed on 1 Oct 1920, and attached to Cavalry Regts 8, 6 (later 2) and 3 respectively. On 15 Sept 1933, they were reorganized into 1st–5th Cavalry Bicycle Bns, each with 4 bicycle coys and a support company. 1st Bn joined 1 Cav Bde, transferring on 29 Sept 1936 to 4 Cav Bde, and on 15 Oct 1937 to 4th Mot (*Motomechanisovana*) Brigade. 2nd Bn joined 2 Cav Bde, then on 15 Oct 1937, 2nd Mot Brigade. 3rd Bn joined 3 Cav Bde, and on 15 Oct 1937, 3rd Mot Bde, while 4th Bn joined 4 Cav Bde, transferring 26 Sept 1936 to 1 Cav Bde, and on 15 Oct 1937 to 1 Mot Brigade. 5th Bn joined 2 Cav Bde, and on 15 Oct 1937, 2nd Mot Brigade.

Mobile Forces

Mobile Divisions. On 1 Jan 1938, the four 11,000-strong 'Mobile Divs' (sing: *Rychlá Divize*; aka 'Fast Divs', and numbered 1–4), were officially operational. They comprised 4 Cav Bdes (numbered 1–4), 4 Mot Bdes (numbered 1–4), an Arty Bde (84, 82, 83, 81 Regts) plus HQ troops. As elite troops, they were engaged in fighting Sudeten German *Freikorps* in 1938.

Mounted Cavalry (*Jezdectvo*). Ten Cavalry Regts were formed on 1 Oct 1920, with 11th Regt added 15 Sept 1933. On 1 Jan 1936, all were redesignated 'Dragoon' regts, and reorganized: 1 Cav Bde (1, 4, 5, 8 & 9 Drgn Regts); 2 Bde (2, 6 & 7); 3 Bde (3, 10 & 11); and 4 Bde added on 1 Oct 1933 (5 & 10). On 1 Sept 1937, Cav Bdes 1–4 joined Mobile Divs 1–4 respectively.

Armoured Cars. 14 company-equivalent and sequentially numbered armoured car squadrons (sing: *Vozatajská eskadrona*) were formed on 15 Sept 1933, with 15–19 Sqns following on 15 Sept 1937. Up to 3 sqns were posted to each of the 11 Cavalry (from 1936, 13 Dragoon) Regiments.

Tanks. The Tank Brigade (*Brigáda útočné vozby*) was formed on 15 Sept 1935 with three sequentially numbered Tank Regts (PÚV), followed in Sept 1938 by 4th Regiment. On 1 Oct 1937, the regts were reorganized as 7 Bns, numbered 1–7. In Sept 1938, the Army had Vz.35 light tanks (in later German use, PzKw 35t) and a handful of Renault FT-17s, plus

Sergey Voytsekhovsky was the only Russian national to reach the rank of *Armádní generál* in the Czechoslovak Army; an infantry officer veteran of the Czechoslovak Legion in Russia, he commanded the Czechoslovak First Army from 27 Sept 1938. Immediately after his forced retirement on 1 Apr 1939, he joined the ON underground resistance (see below, 'The Home Front; Resistance organizations'), but was arrested by the Soviet NKVD, and died in a Soviet prison in Oct 1941. He is shown in 1938 wearing M1930 service dress with combat-arm generals' collar patches; on his right breast, note the wreathed M1923 pilot's qualification 'wings', above a silver 1934 General Staff College graduation badge. (Photographer unknown; Wikimedia Commons/ Public domain)

A Czechoslovak Army general officer wearing an M1930 peaked service cap with double gold twisted chin-cords (which actually appear less bulky than the thick plaited single cord worn by other officers), the gilt badge with crossed 'combat swords', and the peak with gold lime-leaf edging. The M1930 general officer's khaki tunic has bright red collar patches with the M1930 three-leaf gold wire embroidery for combat arms (two leaves for services). His khaki shoulder straps have red outer piping, gold wire inner edging, and a gold wire lime-leaf motif as Table 2, image 4. (Photographer unknown; Wikimedia Commons/Public domain)

about 30 Vz.33 tankettes, but no medium Vz.38s (PzKw 38t) had yet been deployed.

Armoured Trains. From 1925, the Armoured Train Bn *(Obrneny vlak)* comprised six coys, each with a locomotive, pusher wagon, artillery wagon and two machine-gun wagons. A number of improvised rail-cars were also built, which saw some action against *Freikorps* in Sudetenland in 1938.

Artillery

Field Artillery Brigades (sing: *Polnj delostrelecka brigada*). 12 Field Arty Bdes (numbered 1–12) were formed during 1921–37, each comprising three units: 1–12 and 101–112 Field Arty Regts, and 251–262 Field Arty Bns, allocated to 1–12 Inf Divisions. Three more Field Arty Bdes (numbered 13–15) were formed subsequently, each with one Arty Bn (253, 258, 260).

Field Artillery Regiments. 50 Field Arty Regts were numbered 1–15, 18, 19, 51–54, 101–112, 125, 126, 151–154, 201, 205, 301–305, 331 & 356.

Field Artillery Battalions. Four Arty bns were allocated to each Cav Bde, numbered 81 (1 Cav Bde, 1932); 82 (2 Cav Bde, 1938); 83, ex-259 (3 Cav Bde, 1938); and 84 (4 Cav Bde, 1938). 13 ex-Mtn Arty Bns (numbered 251–262, 401) were reorganized on 1 Jan 1923 as Field Arty Bns with the same numbers, but disbanded 1933–38. Four Field Arty bns (numbered 151–154) were reorganized in Oct 1924 as Field Arty Regts with the same numbers. Field Arty Bns 255, 257, 258, 260 & 401 formed Field Arty Bns 81, 82 & 13, and 15 and 401 Field Arty Regts.

Mountain Artillery Regiments. Three (numbered 201, 202, 205) were formed 1 Jan 1923. 205 was disbanded in July 1924, while 201 & 202 became Decontamination Coys (sing: *Asanační rota)* in Mar 1938.

Fortress Artillery. Maginot-style frontier fortifications comprised 264 heavy 'artillery' forts and 10,014 light 'infantry' pillboxes.

Mechanized Transport. One Mech Tspt Regt *(Automobilni pluk)* was formed on 25 Feb 1921, with three Bns (numbered 1–3) fighting as lorried infantry. Four more Bns were later raised: 4th (1 Oct 1935) & 5th–7th Bns (1 Oct 1936), and allocated to Inf Divisions. By Oct 1936, MT troops were operating as 1–15 independent coys under bns carrying the numbers of parent inf divs: 1 Bn (1–5 & 13 Coys); 2 Bn (5–8, 13 & 14 Coys); 3 Bn (9–12, 14 & 15 Coys); 4 Bn (11 & 12 Coys); 5 Bn (3 & 4 Coys); 6 Bn (7 & 8 Coys); 7 Bn (9 & 10 Companies).

Engineers

Engineer Regiments. Five sequentially numbered regts (sing: *Ženijni pluk),* totalling 13 Bns (numbered 1–13), were formed in 1920, and a 6th Regt in 1934. From Oct 1937, they were reorganized as 5 regts, each with 3 Bns (numbered I–III).

Motorized Engineer Companies. Four (sing: *Motorisivana ženijni rota)* were formed in Oct 1937, numbered 11–14, and allocated to four Eng Regts (5, 2, 3 & 1 respectively). Each Coy had 3 Eng Ptns and one MG Platoon. In Oct 1937, the coys were reorganized into 3 Bns: 21 & 22 Bns (5 Eng Regt), and 23 Bn (1 Eng Regiment).

Railway Regiment *(Železniční voysko).* Formed 10 Mar 1919 within the Engineers; initially included 14 Bns, each consisting of one train. Also, from Sept 1933, two Construction Bns (I–II).

1st Motorcycle Regiment. Formed 1 July 1938 from 3 Bns (numbered 21–23) formed 1 Oct 1937, each with two motorcycle coys and a cannon company.

Pontoon Battalion. Formed May 1924 to patrol the Danube on motor-boats. Reorganized Aug 1934 into two Pontoon Coys; redesignated I Bn/4th Eng Regt on 1 Oct 1937.

1st Signal Battalion. Formed 15 Oct 1920; expanded to Signal Regt (I–III Bns) Apr 1921. Seven Signal Bns (numbered 1–7) were formed from 1 Nov 1924 (4 Bn, 15 Aug 1926; 7 Bn, 1 Sept 1935), each with 5 coys (numbered 1–5). 12 Signal Coys were also formed on 1 Nov 1924.

May 1938: Czechoslovak Army mounted machine-gunners (probably from one of the four Mobile Divs) haul their weapon through low cover in the disputed Sudetenland frontier territory, ready to engage German insurgents. They wear M1930 khaki field uniforms with M1932/34 steel helmets, and have gas masks slung on their backs; note too the spurs. At left, a senior private *(svobodník)* shows one silver rank stud on the branch-colour tab at the base of his shoulder straps. (Christopher Harrod Collection)

Air Corps

The Air Corps *(Letecký sbor)* was formed on 30 Oct 1918 as an integral branch of the Army, commanded from Oct 1938 by LtGen Jaroslav Faifr. There were 6 Air Regts (sing: *Letecký pluk*) each with a number of squadrons (sing: *Letka*): 1st Air Regt, formed 6 Sept 1920, Prague (Bohemia); 2nd, formed 6 Sept 1920, Olomouc (Moravia–Silesia); 3rd, formed 6 Sept 1920, Bratislava (Slovakia); 4th, formed 1 Nov 1928, Hradec Králové (Moravia); 5th, formed 1 Oct 1937, Brno (Moravia); and 6th, formed 15 Sept 1929, Kbelich (Moravia). 5th and 6th Air Regts were combined into an Air Brigade *(Letecká brigáda)* from 1 Jan 1934, joined by 4th Regt on 1 Jan 1938. In Sept 1938, the Air Corps fielded some 650 front-line aircraft, mainly Avia B-534 biplane fighters and Letov S-28 reconnaissance and ground-cooperation machines, but including about 60 imported Soviet Tupolev SB-2 monoplane twin-engine bombers.

Services:

Legal Service *(Soudní služba)*. Legal officers were allocated to 11 Div Courts (sing: *Divisní Soud)*.

Chaplain Service *(Duchovní služba)*. Formed 27 Mar 1920 with 36 officers for the Catholic, Protestant, Orthodox and Jewish faiths.

Medical Corps *(Lékárnictvo)*. 12 Div Hospitals (sing: *Divisní nemocnice*) were formed on 1 Mar 1922 (numbered 1–12) and each allocated to a division. On 1 Jan 1937, they were redesignated Corps Hospitals (sing: *Sborovo nemocnice)*, formed 1 Mar 1937 and assigned to Corps Districts as follows: 1, 2 & 5 (I Corps); 3, 4 (II Corps); 6 (III Corps); 7 & 8 (IV Corps); 9 (VII Corps); 10 (V Corps); 11 & 12 (VI Corps).

Medical Orderlies *(Pomocné zdravotnictvo)*. 12 Div Companies were formed on 1 Mar 1922 and allocated to infantry divisions with the same number. In Jan 1937, they were redesignated Corps Coys (sing: *Sborova rota)*.

Veterinary Service *(Veterinárská služba)*. Formed 27 Mar 1920, with 35 stables to service military horses.

Quartermaster Service *(Proviantnictvo; 11 Mar 1930, Intendanční služba)*. 12 Div Warehouses (sing: *Divisní zásobárny*) were formed on 1 Apr 1923, taking divisional numbers. On 1 Jan 1924, they were redesignated Div

16 Mar 1939: a platoon of Italian-built Ansaldo L3/35 tankettes of the Royal Hungarian Army photographed in Chust, Carpathian Ruthenia. The crewmen are wearing M1937 brown leather protective helmets and M1935 brown leather tunics. (Miroslav Hus Collection)

QM Stores (sing: *Divisní proviantní sklad*), and on 1 Jan 1937, Corps QM Stores (sing: *Sborovi proviantní sklad*).

Administrative-Management Service *(Hospodársko-správní služba)*. Redesignated **Administrative Service** *(Intendančni služba)* in Mar 1930.

Engineers Technical Ordnance Service *(Technická zbrojni služba ženijního vojska)*. Formed 1 Aug 1925 to service Engineer equipment.

Air Corps Technical Ordnance Service *(Technická zbrojni služba)*. Formed 1 Aug 1929 to service Air Corps equipment.

UNIFORMS AND INSIGNIA

As a modern democratic republic, Czechoslovakia rejected Austria–Hungary's colourful royalist uniform traditions in favour of a drab uniform with uncomplicated badges and insignia. The first Army uniform was the greenish-grey M1918 pattern introduced on 28 October 1918; this underwent several changes of items and insignia, culminating in the greenish-brown ('British khaki') M1930 pattern, authorized on 22 February 1930 to update the M1921 uniform. Metal items such as buttons, and badges on caps, collars and shoulder straps, were gilt for general officers, field officers and subaltern officers; silver for warrant officers and re-enlisted NCOs; and bronze for other NCOs and enlisted men. Officers and warrant officers wore uniforms in higher-quality materials than the NCOs' and mens' coarser cloth.

Officers' and warrant officers' service and field uniforms, 10 September 1930–30 September 1938

The M1930 peaked cap had branch-colour band piping and a khaki cloth peak. Generals had gold double twisted chin-cords and lime-leaf peak embroidery; officers, and WOs, a thick plaited cord in gold and silver respectively. Combat-arms officers had a gilt cap badge showing a Bohemian Lion on a Shield, on crossed swords, on a diamond shape, and (except for generals) rank badges were displayed on both sides of the cap band.

The Combat Arms' service tunic had buttons with a crossed-swords motif (absent from Services buttons). The tunic had a closed collar with branch-colour collar patches, and metal unit numerals on the shoulder straps; 6 front buttons, two cuff-buttons; point-ended buttoned shoulder straps with branch-colour piping; two external breast pockets with box pleats and scalloped buttoned flaps, and large 'bellows' waist pockets with buttoned flaps. Generals wore two wide bright red trouser stripes flanking red seam piping. A brown leather 'Sam Browne' belt supported a 9mm M1924 pistol in an M1922 holster.

The field uniform differed in only a few particulars. Headgear comprised the greenish-brown painted M1932 (V32/34) steel helmet, and the M1922 field cap (sidecap) with a deep flap, Bohemian Lion badge and rank insignia. M1930 riding breeches were worn with riding boots. The double-breasted greenish-brown M1930 greatcoat had two rows of six buttons and plain cuffs. In addition to the Sam Browne with holstered pistol, an M1923 officer's map-case was also worn.

NCOs' and men's service and field uniforms

The M1930 field sidecap was worn with the M1930 enlisted field tunic. This had bronze buttons, branch-colour patches on a turndown collar, and round-ended shoulder straps piped in branch colours; in line with these, on the collar sides, were bronze unit badges (silver for NCOs). There were 6 front buttons, patch breast pockets with buttoned scalloped flaps, internal waist pockets with diagonal scalloped flaps lacking visible buttons, and plain cuffs. Trousers were worn with khaki puttees and brown leather M1924 ankle boots, and a double-breasted greatcoat was issued.

A brown leather belt was worn, with a brass buckle-plate bearing the Bohemian Lion and Shield. The belt had two sets of paired M1923 rifle ammunition pouches looped to the front. The M1924 backpack, suspended from brown leather belt-support straps, was worn with the M1930 mess tin, a folded tent-section, and an M1925 blanket strapped to it. A water bottle was suspended from the left shoulder to the right hip, and an M1935 gas mask canister was also slung. An M1923 canvas 'breadbag' haversack, an entrenching tool and the frogged M1933 bayonet scabbard hung behind the left hip. The rifle was the 7.92mm M1924 (the Czech-made Mauser ČZ Vz.24).

Branch-specific items

For ceremonial dress, generals and officers wore a brown woven-thread belt with a gilt (WOs, silver) buckle-plate bearing the Bohemian Lion and Shield on lime-leaves. The French, Italian and Russian Representative Coys of the Castle Guard wore modified Czechoslovak Legion uniforms and insignia.

Mounted Cavalry and Armoured Cars wore three tunic cuff-buttons, and traditional Austro–Hungarian bright red riding breeches. Tank crews wore brown leather helmets, khaki overalls with a plain turndown collar, a fly front, plain cuffs and pointed shoulder-straps, and rank stars on a plain patch on the right breast, with a brown leather belt and holster. Tank and armoured car crews could also wear a brown leather tunic and breeches. Artillery crews wore an off-white tunic with breast and waist patch pockets with scalloped flaps, pointed shoulder straps, collar patches and rank insignia, with plain trousers and black leather marching boots.

The Pontoon Bn wore a khaki peakless seaman's cap with a gold, silver or bronze Bohemian Lion badge above rank badges on a branch-colour band with two black hanging ribbons. The M1932 khaki double-breasted pea-jacket was introduced in Aug 1932, with two rows of four buttons, a turndown collar with branch-colour collar patches and anchor side badges, plain cuffs, and internal waist pockets with rectangular flaps. Personnel could also wear the seaman's cap with light blue overalls.

From 13 March 1937, Air Corps officers and WOs wore the M1930 service uniform in greyish-blue cloth, comprising a peaked cap, tunic with open plain collar, trousers and black leather ankle boots. A blue thread belt was worn with their ceremonial order of dress. Aircrew could wear greyish-blue M1933 one-piece flight overalls.

Rank insignia, 16 December 1927–11 May 1945

(*Note:* While Table 2 opposite shows rank insignia specifically from 1937 to 1939, many of the features illustrated were also seen over longer periods.)

General officers wore rank insignia above the cuffs and on the shoulder straps of the M1930 service tunic and greatcoat; other officers and enlisted ranks wore them on the headgear and shoulder straps only. All Combat Arms used the same rank titles, but Services general officers used branch-specific ranks; e.g. *Generál šéf zdravotictva* (Surgeon LtGen), etc. Other officers' rank titles were commonly suffixed with the appropriate branch; e.g. *Plukovník pechote* (Colonel of Infantry).

All officer ranks wore gilt metal buttons; warrant officers and re-enlisted NCOs, silver; and other NCOs and men, bronze.

General officers *(Generali): Armádní generál, Divisní generál, Brigadní generál.* (16 Dec 1927–1943): 4–2 gold wire 5-point cuff rank stars; red shoulder-strap piping.

(1943–11 May 1945) 4–2 stars above crossed swords, on shoulder straps with gold wire edging inside branch-colour piping.

Field officers *(Vyšši důstojnici): Plukovník, Podplukovník, Major, Štábní kapitán.* (22 Feb 1930–11 May 1945) 4–1 gilt metal 5-point stars, on shoulder straps with gold wire edging inside branch-colour piping.

Subaltern officers *(Nizši důstojnici): Kapitán, Nadporučík, Poručík, Podporučík.* (22 Feb 1930–15 Mar 1939) 4–1 gilt metal 3-point stars, on shoulder straps with gold wire edging inside branch-colour piping.

(15 Mar 1939–11 May 1945) 4–1 gilt metal 5-point stars, on shoulder straps with gold wire edging inside branch-colour piping.

Warrant officers *(Rotmistri): Praporčík, Štábní rotmistr, Rotmistr.*

(22 Feb 1930–Oct 1937) 3–1 short silver metal bars, on shoulder straps with 're-enlistment' centre-stripe and piping in branch colour.

(Oct 1937–15 Mar 1939) 3–1 silver metal 3-point stars, on shoulder straps with branch-colour re-enlistment centre-stripe and piping.

(15 Mar 1939–11 May 1945) 4–2 silver metal 5-point stars, on shoulder-straps with branch-colour re-enlistment centre-stripe and piping.

Štábní praporčík (Aug 1938–11 May 1945), 1 silver metal 5-point star, on shoulder straps with silver wire edging, branch-colour centre-stripe and piping.

Non-commissioned officers *(Poddůstojníci): Rotny (délesloužíci), Četar (délesloužíci), Desátník (délesloužíci).*

(22 Feb 1930–1945) Branch-colour piping; 4–2 silver studs, on branch-colour shoulder-strap base tabs. Bronze metal buttons, except for re-enlisted *(délesloužíci)* NCOs, who had silver buttons, and a branch-colour centre-stripe on the shoulder straps.

Men *(Mužstvo): Svobodnik, Vojin.*

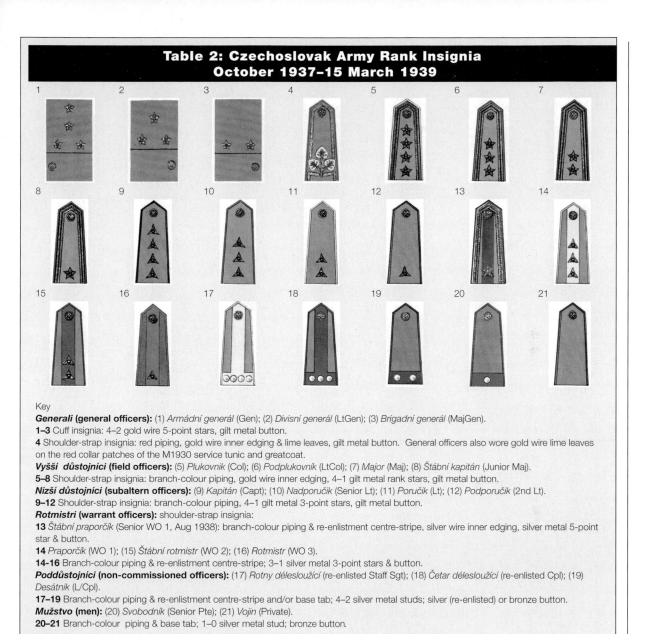

Table 2: Czechoslovak Army Rank Insignia October 1937–15 March 1939

Key

Generali (general officers): (1) *Armádní generál* (Gen); (2) *Divisní generál* (LtGen); (3) *Brigadní generál* (MajGen).
1–3 Cuff insignia: 4–2 gold wire 5-point stars, gilt metal button.
4 Shoulder-strap insignia: red piping, gold wire inner edging & lime leaves, gilt metal button. General officers also wore gold wire lime leaves on the red collar patches of the M1930 service tunic and greatcoat.
Vyšší důstojníci (field officers): (5) *Plukovník* (Col); (6) *Podplukovník* (LtCol); (7) *Major* (Maj); (8) *Štábní kapitán* (Junior Maj).
5–8 Shoulder-strap insignia: branch-colour piping, gold wire inner edging, 4–1 gilt metal rank stars, gilt metal button.
Nizší důstojníci (subaltern officers): (9) *Kapitán* (Capt); (10) *Nadporučik* (Senior Lt); (11) *Poručik* (Lt); (12) *Podporučik* (2nd Lt).
9–12 Shoulder-strap insignia: branch-colour piping, 4–1 gilt metal 3-point stars, gilt metal button.
Rotmistri (warrant officers): shoulder-strap insignia:
13 *Štábní praporčík* (Senior WO 1, Aug 1938): branch-colour piping & re-enlistment centre-stripe, silver wire inner edging, silver metal 5-point star & button.
14 *Praporčík* (WO 1); (15) *Štábní rotmistr* (WO 2); (16) *Rotmistr* (WO 3).
14–16 Branch-colour piping & re-enlistment centre-stripe; 3–1 silver metal 3-point stars & button.
Poddůstojníci (non-commissioned officers): (17) *Rotny délesloužící* (re-enlisted Staff Sgt); (18) *Četar délesloužící* (re-enlisted Cpl); (19) *Desátnik* (L/Cpl).
17–19 Branch-colour piping & re-enlistment centre-stripe and/or base tab; 4–2 silver metal studs; silver (re-enlisted) or bronze button.
Mužstvo (men): (20) *Svobodník* (Senior Pte); (21) *Vojin* (Private).
20–21 Branch-colour piping & base tab; 1–0 silver metal stud; bronze button.

(22 Feb 1930–11 May 1945) 1–0 silver studs, on branch-colour shoulder-strap base tabs; branch-colour shoulder-strap piping. Bronze buttons.

Branch and unit distinctions, 1 January 1930–15 March 1939

All officers wore branch-colour piping on both edges of the band of the M1930 peaked cap, and on the flap of the M1930 peakless field cap (sidecap). Branch colours were displayed on scalloped collar patches (sometimes bearing secondary branch piping, and/or badges; see Table 3, page 14). Shoulder straps were edged with branch-colour piping, and bore a broad branch-colour centre-stripe for WOs and re-enlisted NCOs, and rectangular base tabs for other NCOs and enlisted men. Some personnel wore M1930 metal badges with unit numbers or letters on both sides of the collar in line with the shoulder straps.

Branch and unit:	Collar patches	Shoulder-strap unit number
Combat Arms		
Generals	3 gold lime leaves on large crimson 5-sided patch	None
General Staff officers	Large crimson 5-sided patch	None
62 Infantry Regts	Cherry-red scalloped (3-pointed) patch	9,11,13,16,17,21,27,33,37,41–44,47,51–68,70–78,80–98
1 Castle Guard Bn	Lion & cross on cherry-red scalloped patch	Silver castle
30 Guard Bns	Army, Police & Border Guard insignia	1–3,5–24,29,30,34,36,37,50,51
4 Mountain Inf Regts	Eagle on crag on cherry-red scalloped patch	1–4
6 Border Inf Regts	Dog's head on cherry-red scalloped patch	3–4,6,11,17,18
5 Bicycle Inf Bns	Bicycle wheel on cherry-red scalloped patch	1–5
11 Mounted Cavalry units	Yellow scalloped patch	1–11
19 Armoured Car Sqns	Yellow scalloped patch	1–19
4 Armoured Regts	Arrowhead in ring on cherry-red scalloped patch	1–4
6 Armoured Trains	Scarlet scalloped patch	1–6
40 Field Artillery Regts	Scarlet scalloped patch	1–15,18,19,51–54,101–112,125,126,151–154,201,205,301–305,331,356
8 Field Artillery Bns	Scarlet scalloped patch	81–84,151–154
13 Field Artillery Bns (ex-Mtn)	Scarlet scalloped patch	251–262,401
3 Mountain Artillery Regts	Eagle on crag on cherry-red scalloped patch	201,202,205
Fortress Artillery	Scarlet scalloped patch	Number of original unit
7 Mechanized Transport Regts	Number in ring on scarlet scalloped patch	1–7
6 Engineer Regts	Dark brown scalloped patch	1–6
6 Motorized Engineer Bns	Dark brown scalloped patch	12–14,21–23
1 Motorcycle Regt	Cherry-red scalloped patch	1
1 Railway Regt	Winged wheel on dark brown scalloped patch	1
1 Pontoon Bn	Dark brown scalloped patch	1
7 Signals Bns	Light brown scalloped patch	1–7
6 Air Corps Regts	Light blue scalloped patch	1–6
Services		
Generals	2 gold lime leaves on large 5-sided branch-colour patch	
15 Legal Service Courts	Black velvet scalloped patch	
Chaplains	Large black velvet rectangular patch, piped white	
12 Divisional Hospitals	Black velvet scalloped patch, piped cherry-red	
12 Corps Hospitals	Black scalloped patch, piped cherry-red	1–12
12 Medical Coys	Black scalloped patch	1–15,18,19,201,202
Veterinary officers	Black velvet scalloped patch, piped yellow	
Quartermaster service	Dark blue velvet scalloped patch	
13 Corps QM Stores	Blue velvet scalloped patch	1–13
Administration	Dark blue velvet scalloped patch, piped cherry-red	
Administrative Service	Dark blue velvet scalloped patch	
7 Corps Technical Workshops	Green scalloped patch, piped black	1–7
Signals Technicians	Green scalloped patch, piped light brown	
Aviation Technicians	Green scalloped patch, piped light blue	

THE FALL OF CZECHOSLOVAKIA, 1938–39

German annexation and dissolution

The Sudeten leader Konrad Henlein established various paramilitary organizations inspired by their German equivalents, the most important being the Volunteer Protection Service (*Freiwilliger Schutzdienst* – FS). Formed on 14 May 1938 as an internal security force, this eventually boasted 60,000–70,000 members. On 16 September 1938, it was absorbed by the 41,000-strong Sudeten German Free Corps (*Sudetendeutsches Freikorps*), which waged a cross-border war with Czechoslovakian forces during 18–30 September 1938.

Political tension had led to the Czechoslovak government announcing a partial Army mobilization on 20 May 1938. No German attack materialized, but 1st Mobile and part of 4th Mobile Divs saw action against Sudeten German insurgents. Responding to the continuing international crisis, Czechoslovakia fully mobilized on 23 September, but the country was abandoned to its fate by French and British government diplomats at the Munich Conference. On 30 September, Prime Minister Gen Jan Syrový signed the Munich Agreement, which ceded Sudetenland to Germany, including the fortifications essential for Czechoslovakia's defence. Armed resistance was minimal, and only III Bn/8th Border Regt defended their positions when German troops entered Sudetenland from 5 October onwards.

On 1 October 1938, Konrad Henlein was appointed 'Imperial Commissioner and Provincial Leader of Sudetenland Imperial Province' (*Reichskommissar und Gauleiter der Reichgau Sudetenland*). On 15 March 1939, German forces occupied the rest of what then became Germany's 'Protectorate of Bohemia and Moravia' with Henlein's ostensible role as Imperial Commissioner territorially extended. On 21 March, the German Foreign Minister, Konstantin von Neurath, was appointed Protectorate Governor (*Reichsprotektor*). He nominally held this post until 9 May 1945, but in fact lost his practical authority from 29 September 1941, when Hitler appointed SS LtGen Reinhard Heydrich as Acting Governor (*Stellvertretender Reichsprotektor*), to be followed by SS Gen Kurt Daluege on 4 June 1942 following Heydrich's assassination (see below – 'The Home Front: The SOE and Operation 'Anthropoid').

Ruthenia, 1938–39

Ruthenia is an ancient traditional name for a region, much reduced in the 20th century, which lay between Hungary, Slovakia, Ukraine and Romania. Hungary had long harboured ambitions to recover its lost territories, and immediately exploited the Munich Agreement to secure German backing. Premature incursions by members of Hungary's irregular 'Ragged Guard' were defeated, but on 2 November 1938, Germany and Italy granted Hungary mainly Magyar-ethnic territories in southern Slovakia and southern Ruthenia, which were occupied by the Royal Hungarian Army over the following week.

With Hitler's encouragement, Slovakia declared its independence (under German control) from Bohemia–Moravia on 14 March 1939, and on the same day Subcarpathian Ruthenia (also called Subcarpathian Rus, and located in eastern Slovakia and northern Ruthenia) followed suit, proclaiming a Republic of Carpatho–Ukraine. On 15 March, the once-formidable Czechoslovak Army was officially abolished; however, its understrength 12th Inf Div, garrisoning Subcarpathian Ruthenia, refused to disband. Commanded by MajGen Oleg Svátek and based at Chust (now Khust, Ukraine), it had only some 3,000 men from 2 infantry regiments, 2 artillery battalions, armoured car and motorcycle companies and other units, including 2 SOS battalions.

On 14 March, Hungary's 15,000-strong Carpathian Corps *(Karpátcsoport)*, with 1 Mot and 2 Cav Bdes plus reinforcements, advanced northwards and engaged Czechoslovak forces in Mukachevo (now in Ukraine). General Svátek informed his Corps HQ in Prešov of the Hungarian attack, but was denied support by newly independent and hostile Slovakia. The 12th Inf Div was also threatened by advancing German forces. On 15 March, Svátek divided his troops into three groups: Western and Central Groups headed westwards to Slovakia, and the Eastern Group southwards to Romania. The Czechoslovaks executed a successful fighting retreat as ordered. The Hungarians did not reach the Polish border until 16 March, or seal it until 20 March. Western and Central Groups surrendered to the Slovak Army and were evacuated to Bohemia–Moravia by train during 20–23 March, whilst the Eastern Group reached home via Romania and Yugoslavia. This had been the last battle of the pre-1939 Czechoslovak Army. Meanwhile, Carpatho–Ukraine's 2,000-strong Carpathian Defence Force *(Karpatski Sič)* was easily defeated by the Slovaks during 13–15 March.[2]

The Czech and Slovak Legion, September 1939

From April 1939, patriotic groups crossed the Polish border at Moravsa Ostrava; many gathered in the Kraków Consulate and Warsaw Embassy, where Polish officials defied German demands by allowing Czechs to emigrate to France. On 30 April, about 52 former Czechoslovak Army personnel commanded by Air Corps Lt Jiří Král formed the 'Foreign Military Czechoslovak Group' *(Zahraniční vojenska skupina – ZVS)* in Kraków, planning to serve in the Polish Army. On 6 June 1939, LtCol Ludvík Svoboda, a pro-Soviet communist, was appointed commander, but he emigrated to the Soviet Union in late June. On 7 July, the Polish authorities, concerned that the ZVS might provoke German retribution, interned them in camps at Bronowice Małé and Leśna near Kraków. Some 200 ground and 93 flying personnel of the Air Corps were also assembled in Dęblin.

France agreed to accept 477 Czechoslovak servicemen and 743 civilians, but between 22 May and 21 August, six ships in fact transported about 4,000 Czechoslovaks from Gdynia to France, leaving about 1,000 in the Bronowice Małé camp. In Poland, the outbreak of war on 3 September 1939 led to 630 Czechoslovaks being formally organized as the 'Czechoslovak Legion' *(Československá legie)* or 'Czech and Slovak

---

2   See also MAA 449, *The Royal Hungarian Army in World War II*.

Legion' (Česká a slovenská legie), commanded by Gen Lev Prchala. This battalion-strength force officially comprised the embryos of an infantry battalion, artillery battalion, tank company, armoured car platoon, air squadron, and a reserve battalion. The Czechoslovaks were issued Polish khaki Army and greyish-blue Air Force M1936 uniforms, and were based at Tarnopol, Poland (now Ternopil, Ukraine). On 11 September, the 725-strong Legion began an orderly retreat from the advancing Germans, but on 19 September, most were captured by Red Army troops at Rakowiec, and subsequently interned in Suzdal and Oranki camps near Moscow. On 22 September 1939, Gen Prchala retreated into Romania with survivors of the Legion and some Air Corps personnel.

WITH THE WESTERN ALLIES, 1939–45

Czechoslovaks in the French Army, 1939–40

From 20 May 1939, many Czechoslovaks resident in France enlisted in the French Foreign Legion, joining the 1st and 2nd Foreign Inf Regts (1er & 2e REIs), and in 1940 the 13th Foreign Legion Half-Brigade (13e DBLE). Following the outbreak of war on 3 September 1939, most Czechoslovak volunteers transferred to the French Army, although some remained in the Legion and/or subsequently joined the Free French forces.

Members of the 1st Czechoslovak Inf Div equipped with French Army khaki uniforms, 1940. The khaki-painted M1926 Adrian helmets lack a frontal plate; the M1938 tunics, with 5 front buttons, have turndown collars with khaki tabs to conceal French branch-colour unit numerals and pipings, and internal waist pockets with buttonless diagonal flaps. No French or Czechoslovak insignia are visible. The baggy M1938 trousers are worn with khaki puttees and brown ankle boots, and the belt equipment is brown leather. They carry 7.5mm French MAS36 bolt-action rifles. (Associated Press via Alamy)

France, July 1940: LtGen Sergĕj Ingr (centre), Chief of General Staff, with Polish and British officers. He wears an M1933 peaked cap with general officers' distinctions. His greatcoat has 3 gold rank stars above the cuffs; red-piped, gold-edged shoulder straps; and, already, new red-on-khaki 'CZECHOSLOVAKIA' shoulder titles. (Lt J.R. Bainbridge/Wikimedia Commons/Public domain)

Palestine, Oct 1940: Czechoslovak infantrymen 'presenting arms' to a British general with .303in SMLE rifles. They wear British tropical 'aertex' shirts and long 'khaki drill' (KD) shorts, with M1938 'solar topee' helmets, and stripped M1908 webbing belts. (Nigel Thomas Collection)

On 20 October 1939, President Beneš and LtGen Sergĕj Ingr established the 'Reformed Czechoslovak Army in France' at Béziers, with Czechoslovak residents, exiles, and légionnaires. On 15 January 1940, LtGen Rudolf Viest formed the 11,405-strong 1st Czechoslovak Inf Div at Agde, to be commanded by BrigGen Jan Kratochvíl. The formation comprised an HQ and support units; Cav & MT sqns; 1st & 2nd Inf Regts (I–III Bns each) and a partially formed 3rd Inf Regt; 1st Arty Regt (I–III Bns), and Eng and Sigs battalions.

During the Battle of France, May–June 1940, the 1st Czechoslovak Div fought well at Coulommiers on the Marne River and at Gien on the Loire, but was ordered to retreat to avoid being outflanked. The 1st & 2nd Inf Regts were then attached to the French 23rd Inf Div and 239th Lt Inf Div respectively. On 13 June, under attack by German armour, the Czechoslovaks were forced to retreat southwards past Orléans and Tours. On 26 June, the remaining 3,500 men arrived at the Mediterranean port of Sète, just in time to board British ships that evacuated them to Liverpool.

With the British Army: the Middle East, 1940–43

The Franco–German Armistice of 22 June 1940 found 206 Czech volunteers trapped in Vichy-ruled Beirut, Lebanon, while awaiting transfer to the Czechoslovak division in France. J.M. Kadlec, the Czechoslovak consul-general in Jerusalem, promptly obtained visas allowing them to cross into British-controlled Palestine. The Czechoslovaks, soon 280 strong, were housed in a camp at Al-Sumeirya, where they became 4th Inf Regt, Czechoslovak Inf Div, with an HQ, Maintenance Coy, and an Inf Regt with two complete and two cadre companies.

On 23 July 1940, the British government recognized the London-based Czechoslovak government-in-exile, and that September about 1,000 Czechoslovak troops interned by the Soviets were permitted to travel via Romania to Palestine, where on 1 October the 'Czechoslovak Contingent to the Near and Middle East' was formed under LtGen Ondrej Mezl. The 4th Inf Regt was re-formed as Czechoslovak Inf Bn No 11 (East) and a Czechoslovak Training Depot (East) was established. By November 1940, the British-sponsored Czechoslovak Army had 3,470 men plus 1,250 airmen in the Royal Air Force, making the Czechoslovak contingent second only to the Poles among Britain's foreign allies.

Infantry Bn No 11 was commanded by LtCol Karel Klapálek, with a Bn HQ, 4 Rifle coys (each with 3 ptns) and a Support coy comprising MG, Sigs, Eng repair and Tspt platoons. From early December 1940, the Bn performed training and guard duties at Sidi Bishr and Agami camps until 30 May 1941, when it joined the British 23rd Inf Bde (of 4th Indian Div) near Mersa Matruh, Egypt. It fought with 23 Bde in the unsuccessful Operation 'Battleaxe' in Libya, then in the successful occupation of Vichy-held Lebanon and Syria in Operation 'Exporter' in June–July

1941, before guarding the Syrian border with Turkey. The British refused Czechoslovak requests to transfer the unit to Great Britain, instead sending it on 6 October 1941 to the besieged Libyan port of Tobruk as part of the replacements for the tired Australian garrison. There, under the Polish Gen Kopanski's Indep Carpathian Rifle Bde, it maintained a line of fortlets and pill boxes defending the vulnerable western perimeter. By the time of the break-out by the 'Rats of Tobruk' on 7/8 December, the Czechoslovaks had been in the front line for 51 days.

Pulled back, in March 1942 the 11th Inf Bn was subordinated to the British 4th AA Bde at Haifa, Palestine, and on 21 April 1942 it was reorganized as the 200th Czechoslovak Light AA Regt (East) with 1,547 men, including some overseas conscripts. Commanded by Col Klapálek, the 200th had 3 bns (numbered 500–502), each with 4 coys (numbered sequentially 1–12), a Sigs ptn and a Repair section. On 21 July 1942, the regiment was assigned to the defence of Haifa and later Beirut ports, and from December 1942 to July 1943, it returned to Tobruk under the British 17th Brigade. Finally, on 4 July 1943, the regiment – totalling 1,333 men – left the port of Tewfik to arrive in Liverpool on 11 August, its personnel subsequently joining the Czechoslovak Indep Armd Bde (see below, 'Great Britain & NW Europe, 1940–45'). During the Middle East campaign, the Czechoslovaks had lost 38 soldiers killed in action.

Members of the 11th Infantry Bn (East) manning a gunpit in Tobruk, Libya, on 24 Oct 1941. They now wear British Mk II helmets and M1937 web equipment – compare with Plate C3. (Czech 11th Battalion Tobruk 1941/Wikimedia Commons/ Public domain)

The Far East, 1941–42

Before World War II, hundreds of Czechoslovaks, including businessmen, journalists and engineers, lived in the Far East, and were mostly organized in Czechoslovak expatriate associations. From September 1939, some enlisted in the army in exile in France or Lebanon, but most remained in the Far East and joined local part-time territorial units raised by the colonial powers to resist the expected Japanese invasions.

The Czechoslovak contingent had luckily been posted elsewhere by the time Tobruk's second siege ended with the surrender of the mainly South African garrison on 21 June 1942. Here, men of the redesignated 200th Czechoslovak Light AA Regt (East) guard the perimeter of Haifa, Palestine, in August 1942. (IWM)

A Czechoslovak platoon of the Shanghai Volunteer Corps on a march through the Hong Kong countryside, 1940, wearing British service dress with SVC cap badges. Officers (e.g. the young Czechoslovak at left) wore superior-quality M1902 SD caps, M1912 open-collar SD tunics with SVC collar badges, Sam Browne belts, trousers and brown shoes, plus here a double-breasted khaki greatcoat. The enlisted men wore British M1902 SD caps with closed-collar M1902 tunics (sometimes with collar badges), trousers, puttees, black 'ammunition boots' and web belts. WO Class 1s wore officers'-quality tunics with closed collars, and Sam Brownes; NCOs displayed point-down white chevrons on both upper sleeves. (Photographer unknown; Wikimedia Commons/Public domain)

The largest of these was the Shanghai Volunteer Corps, formed as long ago as 1857, which by 1941 had about 20 national companies and battalions. The Czechoslovak Coy was formed in December 1941 as part of the British Bn, but was defeated in Hong Kong during 8–25 December and mostly taken prisoner. The Volunteer Defence Corps (VDC) was an Australian Home Guard, recruiting across the Far East, which would grow to 111 battalions in 1944. A Czechoslovak platoon which was formed within its Scottish MG Coy fought with distinction in Hong Kong, later enduring cruel captivity in Sham Shui Po Camp until the Japanese surrender.

Members of the Czechoslovak government-in-exile visit Northern Ireland, 1942. (Foreground, left to right:) BrigGen Edmund Hill, US Army; Gen Ingr, Minister of Defence and C-in-C Czechoslovak Forces; LtGen Harold Franklyn, GOC British Troops in Northern Ireland; AVM Janoušek, Inspector-General Czechoslovak Air Force; and Jan Masaryk, Foreign Minister and Deputy Prime Minister. (IWM)

(continued on page 29)

INTERNAL SECURITY, 1938–39
1: *Armádni gen* Syrový
2: *Četar délesloužící,* 3rd Inf Regt
3: *Strážmistr,* Liberec Bn, State Defence Guard

A

FRANCE, 1939–40
1: *Kapitán* Alois Vašátko, GC I/5, May 1940
2: *Štábní kapitán,* 1st Arty Regt, 1st Czechoslovak Div, June 1940
3: *Vojin,* 2nd Inf Regt, 1st Czechoslovak Div

B

WITH THE BRITISH ARMY, 1940–42
1: *Podporučik,* 1st Inf Bn; Cheshire, 1940
2: *Praporčík,* 11th Inf Bn; Lebanon, July 1941
3: *Rotny aspirant,* 11th Inf Bn; Tobruk, Dec 1942

C

WITH THE BRITISH ARMY, 1942–45
1: *Rotmistr* Jan Kubiš; SOE, London, May 1942
2: *Četar,* 1st Czechoslovak Indep Armd Bde; Normandy, Aug 1944
3: *Brigádní gen* Liška, 1st CIAB; Dunkirk, Oct 1944

D

WITH THE RED ARMY, 1941–45
1: *Svobodník*, 1st Czechoslovak Indep Bn; Buzuluk, Apr 1942
2: *Rotny*, 1st Czechoslovak Indep Armd Bde; Dukla Pass, Sept 1944
3: *Brigadní gen* Príkryl, 2nd Czechoslovak Indep Para Bde, 1945

E

PROTECTORATE GOVT ARMY, 1944–45
1: *Rotny,* 2nd Bn; Italy, June 1944
2: *Hejtman I tríedy,* 3rd Bn; Italy, June 1944
3: *Praporčík,* 1st Czechoslovak Bde; Italy, Apr 1945

LIBERATION OF PRAGUE, MAY 1945
1: Civilian insurgent
2: *Podstrázmistr*, Protectorate Gendarmerie
3: *Štábní strážmistr,* Protectorate State Police

In early 1941, about 40 Czechoslovak employees of the Bata shoe factory in Malaya formed a platoon in the 1st Bn Straits Settlements Volunteer Force. That November, they were transferred to British units, distinguishing themselves at Gab Hill and in other battles. Later, 37 Czechoslovaks were imprisoned in Changi Camp, and some worked as slave labourers on the infamous Burma Railway.

India had a large Czechoslovak expatriate population. Most were employed in war industries but some volunteered for the British Army, serving in the RAMC, REME, Indian Air Force and other combat branches. Czechoslovaks in the Philippines formed a platoon with the US Army in January 1942; some surrendered in April at Bataan (most

After VE-Day, 8 May 1945, off-duty soldiers of the Czechoslovak Indep Armd Bde pose on a Cromwell Mk IV tank at La Panne near Dunkirk; note the brigade sign left of the hull machine gun. The brigade's Cromwells were supported by a number of 17pdr Sherman Fireflies and Challengers for longer-range firepower, and light M5 Stuarts for reconnaissance. The men are wearing M1937 and M1940 British battledress with shirt, tie and open collar; they carry no equipment or weapons, and at least one seems to have his webbing belt 'blancoed' white, presumably for the victory celebrations. The five-man tank crew wear Royal Armoured Corps M1941 black berets with Bohemian Lion and Shield badges, while men of the Motor Inf Bn have M1943 khaki General Service caps. (Czech 11th Battalion Tobruk 1941/Wikimedia Commons/Public domain)

subsequently dying on the 'Death March'), and in May on Corregidor. More of them perished in Cabanatuan Camp, but a few evaders fought on with Filipino guerrillas.

Great Britain and NW Europe, 1940–45

In early June 1940, the remnant of the 1st Czechoslovak Inf Div arrived at Cholmondeley (pron. 'Chumley') Park, near Chester in Cheshire, coming under the authority of the exile MNO in London. On 21 July, LtGen Ingr was appointed Minister of War, with LtGen Viest as his deputy. On 12 August, the former division was redesignated 1st Czechoslovak Mixed Brigade (1. Československá Smíšená Brigáda), commanded by MajGen Bogumil Miroslav; it numbered 3,274 men in 1st & 2nd Inf Bns, AT, MG, MT, and support companies, and services.

The brigade remained in Great Britain undergoing training for four years. Relocating to Leamington Spa in October 1940, it added a 3rd Inf Bn, 2nd Arty Bn and an AA Battery. On 1 July 1941, it was redesignated the Czechoslovak Indep Bde (Československá Samostatná Brigáda). In May 1942, it transferred to Ilminster, Somerset, and that August to Lowestoft, Suffolk (where Col Kratochvíl was appointed commanding officer on 25 July 1943). Subsequent moves were to Harwich, Essex, and (1 Sept 1943) to Arthingworth, Northamptonshire, where it was redesignated Czechoslovak Independent Armoured Brigade (Československá Sāmostatná Obrnená Brigáda) under MajGen Alois Liška, with Col Klapálek as 2iC. There were 4,046 men in the 1st & 2nd (plus from 10 March 1945, 3rd) Armd Bns (each 3 coys); 1st Mot Inf Bn (3 coys); Arty Regt (2, later 3 btys); AT Bn; Eng Bn (2, later 3 coys); support units and services. In May 1944, the Bde transferred to Galashiels, Scottish Borders.

On 30 August 1944, the Czechoslovak Independent Armd Bde, now fully trained and 5,676 strong, joined the First Canadian Army at Falaise, Normandy. It then laid siege to the strategic German-held port of Dunkirk for seven months (8 Oct 1944–11 May 1945), ending three days after VE-Day. The brigade then returned to Czechoslovakia, but Gen Liška's triumphant entry into Prague on 18 May was upstaged by Gen Svoboda's 1st Czechoslovak Corps from the USSR, which had occupied the capital several days earlier. On arrival in Prague, Liška's brigade was formally absorbed into the post-war Czechoslovak Army.

Air Corps

In 1939, aircrew who had escaped from Czechoslovakia were dispersed at 20 different locations across France, having joined nine French squadrons. Personnel wore dark blue French Armée de l'Air uniforms with Czechoslovak insignia. The top Czechoslovak ace in the Battle of France was Capt Alois Vašátko, a Curtiss Hawk pilot credited with at least 12 'kills' (see Plate B1).

On 18 June 1940, as France collapsed, Col Karel Janoušek led a large group of Czechoslovak airmen into exile in Great Britain. On 12 July, a Czechoslovak Air Force Inspectorate was established with the promoted Air Vice Marshal Janoušek as Inspector-General. Three Czechoslovak fighter squadrons were subsequently formed in the RAFVR: 310 Sqn and 312 Sqn (formed 12 July 1940) at Duxford with Hawker Hurricanes, later Supermarine Spitfires, and 313 Sqn (10 May 1941) at Catterick with Spitfires. In May 1942, these squadrons formed the Czechoslovak (later No 134) Fighter Wing. Meanwhile, No 311 (Bomber) Sqn was formed on 29 July 1940 with Vickers Wellingtons, later receiving B-24 Liberators; and a flight of No 68 (Night-Fighter) Sqn flew in other Polish and RAF squadrons with Bristol Beaufighters, later De Havilland Mosquitoes. The leading RAF air ace in the Battle of Britain was a Czechoslovak, Josef František, who joined the Czechoslovak Air Corps in 1934, the Polish Air Force in September 1939, and the RAF's No 303 (Polish) Sqn on 8

Fighter pilots of the RAF's No 310 (Czechoslovak) Sqn photographed after being decorated by Dr Edvard Beneš, the Czechoslovak president-in-exile, at Exeter on 18 July 1942. The airmen, all commissioned, wear greyish-blue RAF uniforms and RAF rank insignia, most with SD peaked caps but some with Field Service sidecaps. Volunteers (including the Czechoslovaks) wore a brass 'VR' (Volunteer Reserve) on both collars, and these pilots display light blue M1940 'CZECHOSLOVAKIA' shoulder titles on arc-shaped greyish-blue backing. They have just received awards of the Czechoslovak War Cross 1939 and/or the War Participation Medal 1940. (IWM)

August 1940 as a sergeant pilot. Commissioned during September, he flew Hurricanes with a skill that earned him toleration of his undisciplined 'lone wolf' tactics. Before his fatal crash on 3 October, he was credited with 17 confirmed kills and one 'probable' (8 of them, Messerschmitt Bf 109 fighters). František was awarded the Czechoslovak War Cross, Polish Virtuti Militari, French Croix de Guerre and British Distinguished Flying Medal.

WITH THE RED ARMY, 1941–45

From Battalion to Army Corps

On 22 June 1941, the date of Hitler's invasion of the Soviet Union, Edvard Beneš, president of the Czechoslovak government-in-exile in London, authorized the establishment of Czechoslovak military units in the Soviet Union from the 'Eastern Group of the Czechoslovak Army' (scarcely 100 strong), who had been interned for 30 months. A unit was officially mobilized on 12 February 1942 at Buzuluk in the Ural Mountains, as 1st Czechoslovak Independent Field Battalion in the USSR (*1. Československy Samostatny Polní Prapor v SSSR*). Colonel Ludvík Svoboda commanded 974 men in 1st–3rd Inf Coys; MG, AT and Mortar coys, and support services. On 1 February 1943, a 1st Czechoslovak Reserve Regt was added.

The unit first saw action on 8–13 March 1943 at Sokolovo, near Kharkov (now Kharkiv), Ukraine, where it distinguished itself in delaying

Members of the '1st Indep Field Bn in the USSR', Feb 1942. They wear British battledress with a mixture of Czechoslovak or British FS caps and Red Army M1931 *finska* fleece caps. Footwear is equally mixed, between British web anklets and ankle boots, and Russian marching boots. They are armed with SMLE rifles, and their Czechoslovak brown leather belts have two sets of paired rifle ammunition pouches.
(Nigel Thomas Collection)

a German advance on the Mrzha river. On 12 June 1943, the Bn and Reserve Regt were combined as the 1st Czechoslovak Indep Bde in the USSR *(1. Československá Samostatná Brigáda v SSSR)*, with 1st & 2nd Inf Bns; 1st & 2nd Arty Bns, Armd and AA Battalions. The only non-Soviet unit fighting in the Red Army at that time, it was well armed but lacked sufficient armoured vehicles; nevertheless, it gained prestige by its advance into Kyiv on 5 November 1943. The Bde then continued through Central Ukraine, via Vasylkiv, Fastiv, Bilou Cerkev (1 January 1944) and Žaškov (northern Slovakia). This allowed it to recruit some 2,000 Slovak Army deserters and 12,000 West Ukrainian Czechoslovaks from Rivne district.

On 8 April 1944, the Bde halted on the Polish side of the strategic Dukla Pass on the Polish–Slovak border, unable to advance further into Slovakia. On 5 May, it was reorganized as the 1st Czechoslovak Army Corps in the USSR *(1. Československy Armádní Sbor v SSSR)* under MajGen Jan Kratochvíl, with 16,000 men in four brigades: 1st Indep Bde (1st–3rd Inf Bns); 1st Mech Bde (1st Arty, 1st AT, 1st AA Bns); 2nd Indep Parachute Bde (1st & 2nd Para, 2nd Arty, 2nd AT, 2nd AA Bns, services), formed 20 Jan 1944 from the Slovak Mobile Div; 3rd Indep Bde (4th & 5th Inf, 2nd Mech, 3rd Arty, 4th AT, 3rd AA Bns, services); and 1st Indep Armd Bde (1st Armd Bn, services), formed on 25 July 1944.

The Slovak uprising

On 29 August 1944, the Slovak Army rebelled against German forces at Banská Bystrica. The Czechoslovak Army Corps tried to capture the Dukla Pass to relieve the Slovaks, but were repelled with heavy losses. On 10 September 1944, the commander of the Soviet 1st Ukrainian Front, Marshal Ivan Konev, controversially dismissed Gen Kratochvíl, replacing him with a fellow communist, Gen Svoboda.

Soldiers of the expanded '1st Czechoslovak Indep Bde in the USSR', Ukraine, March 1944. They wear British Mk II helmets with battledress uniform, web anklets and ankle boots. They still have Czechoslovak belt equipment, but the rifles are now 7.62mm M1891 Mosin-Nagants with fixed bayonets. Two junior officers (left) are identifiable by belts with single cross braces, black leather marching boots, and holstered pistols on their right hips. See title page for photo of more Soviet-issue items in 1945. (Nigel Thomas Collection)

On 7 October 1944, the 2,200-strong 2nd Indep Para Bde dropped behind German lines into Banská Bystrica, accompanied by MajGen Rudolf Viest, who was appointed commander of the internal partisan forces now designated '1st Czechoslovak Army in Slovakia' *(1. Československá Armáda u Slovensku)*. The Czechoslovak Army Corps took the Dukla Pass the same day, but too late to save the Slovak insurgency, which finally surrendered on 31 October.

On 5 February 1945, a 4th Indep Para Bde (7th–9th Inf, 3rd Mech, 7th Arty, 4th AA Bns, services) was organized, and joined the Army Corps as a re-formed 2nd Para Brigade. The first units of the 31,325-strong Czechoslovak Army Corps reached Prague on 10 May 1945, in time to help Czechoslovak internal forces defeat the last Germans the following day (see below, 'The battle for Prague').

Air Corps

The 1st Czechoslovak Fighter Air Regt was formed in April 1944 as the air element of 1st Czechoslovak Army Corps in the USSR. It was expanded in January 1945 into the 1st Czechoslovak Mixed Air Div, with 1st & 2nd Fighter Air Regts equipped with Lavochkin LA-5 fighters, and 3rd Assault Air Regt with Ilyushin Il-2 *Sturmovik* ground-attack aircraft. Czechoslovak Army uniforms and insignia were worn.

THE HOME FRONT, 1939–45

Bohemia–Moravia Protectorate Government Army

The Government Army *(Vládní Vojsko)* was established by the German authorities on 25 July 1939, as a modest military force for internal security duties in the Bohemia–Moravia Protectorate. It consisted of about 7,000 volunteers on 12-year enlistments, 280 officers (including 5 generals), and 280 military officials.

Major-General (1 Aug 1942, Gen) Jaroslav Erminger commanded the Inspectorate-General *(Generální Inspektorát)*, which was divided into three District Inspectorates (sing: *Oblastní Inspektorát)*, with a total of 12 battalions varying between 480 and 540 strong. A Bn had 3 Coys – 1st Inf, 2nd Motorcycle, and 3rd Mounted Cav – each with 3 Ptns, and a 4th Technical Coy with Eng, Sigs, auxiliary and band platoons. Deployments

Early 1945: a tank crew of the '1st Independent Czechoslovak Armd Bde in the USSR' pose in front of their 1942-production T-34, wearing Red Army protective tank helmets and the M1944 khaki uniform (see Plate E2). These soldiers seem too tired to be much impressed by the Czechoslovak War Crosses 1939 and War Participation Medals 1940 which they have just been awarded. (Nigel Thomas Collection)

General *(Generál I triedy)* Jaroslav Erminger, Inspector-General of the Protectorate Government Army, photographed in Jan 1943 (compare with Plate F1 and Table 4, image 1). Here he is wearing the khaki M1939 service tunic; the large, 5-sided 'notched' red shoulder straps are covered with gold-embroidered lime leaves, and the red collar patches with lime-branch embroidery behind three gold 5-point rank stars. His dark brown braid officers' ceremonial belt has gilt metal fittings. (Nigel Thomas Collection)

were as follows: *Generální Inspektorát* (Prague). *Inspektorát I* (Benešov): 1 Bn (Prague Castle Guard), 2 Bn (Rakovník, Kralovice), 3 Bn (Písek, Tyn-nad-Vitou), 4 Bn (Benešov), 5 Bn (Kutná Hora, Čáslav). *Inspektorát II* (Josefov): 6 Bn (Hradec Králové), 7 Bn (Josefov), 8 Bn (Jičín), 11 Bn (Kostelec). *Inspektorát III* (Bučovice): 9 Bn (Vysoké Mýto), 10 Bn (Bučovice), 12 Bn (Lipník).

Uniforms and insignia

The Government Army's 'M1939' uniform (25 July 1939 to late 1940) was essentially the Czechoslovak Army M1930 uniform with altered insignia, as described below. From late 1940 to 4 October 1944, a modified sequence of insignia was worn, hereafter the 'M1940' insignia as illustrated in Table 4 opposite.

The M1939 uniform was distinguished by a tricolour cap cockade (white outer, red, blue centre). Rank insignia comprised gilt metal collar stars and embroidered lime leaves on collar patches in three branch colours: red for general officers, yellow for combat arms, and lime-green for military officials. Silver Arabic Bn (1–12) or Roman Inspectorate numbers (I–III) were worn on the shoulder straps below/outside branch badges.

M1939, General officers *(Generali). General III – I triedy:* 3–1 gold 5-point stars and 3 gold lime leaves and branches on red 'notched'(5-sided) collar patches. (**M1940,** unchanged.)

M1939, Field officers *(Vyšší důstojníci). Plukovník, Podplukovník & Major:* 3–1 gold 5-point stars and 2 gold lime leaves and branches on branch-

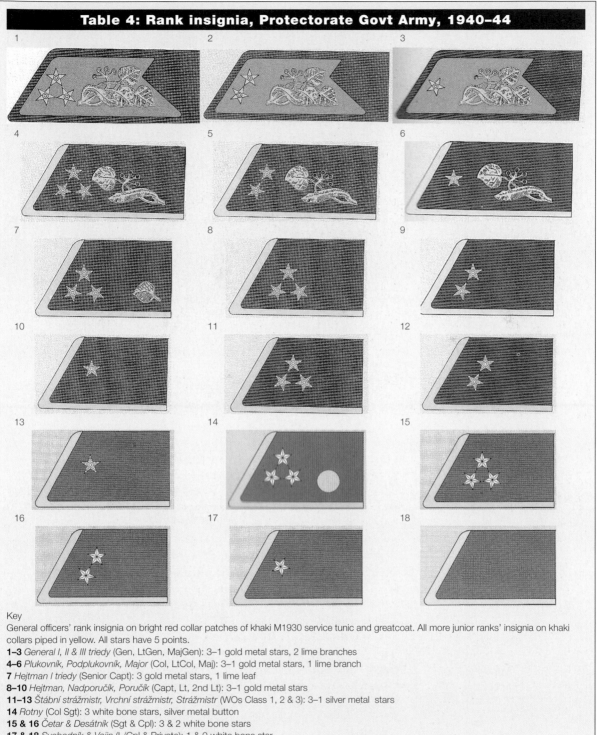

Table 4: Rank insignia, Protectorate Govt Army, 1940-44

Key

General officers' rank insignia on bright red collar patches of khaki M1930 service tunic and greatcoat. All more junior ranks' insignia on khaki collars piped in yellow. All stars have 5 points.

1-3 *General I, II & III triedy* (Gen, LtGen, MajGen): 3-1 gold metal stars, 2 lime branches
4-6 *Plukovník, Podplukovník, Major* (Col, LtCol, Maj): 3-1 gold metal stars, 1 lime branch
7 *Hejtman I triedy* (Senior Capt): 3 gold metal stars, 1 lime leaf
8-10 *Hejtman, Nadporučík, Poručík* (Capt, Lt, 2nd Lt): 3-1 gold metal stars
11-13 *Štábní strážmistr, Vrchní strážmistr, Strážmistr* (WOs Class 1, 2 & 3): 3-1 silver metal stars
14 *Rotny* (Col Sgt): 3 white bone stars, silver metal button
15 & 16 *Četar & Desátník* (Sgt & Cpl): 3 & 2 white bone stars
17 & 18 *Svobodník & Vojin* (L/Cpl & Private): 1 & 0 white bone star.

colour 5-sided collar patches. (**M1940,** no collar patches; insignia worn on khaki collar with branch-colour piping.)
M1939, Subaltern officers *(Nizší důstojníci).*
Hejtman I triedy: 3 gold 5-point stars and 1 gold lime leaf on branch-colour 5-sided collar patches.

Josef Ježek was a Czechoslovak major-general who commanded the Protectorate Gendarmerie *(Generál četnictva)* from 16 Mar 1939 to 9 May 1945. He retained this command even after being dismissed as Minister of the Interior in Jan 1942 for refusing to swear an oath of loyalty; like many police officials, Ježek was a secret member of the ON resistance. The Gendarmerie uniform was similar to the Army's but made of dark greenish-grey cloth, with red cap band, collar patches, shoulder-strap piping and centre-stripes. (Zamberské listy/Wikimedia Commons/Public domain)

Hejtman, Nadporučík, Poručík: 3–1 gold 5-point stars on same collar patches. (**M1940,** no collar patches; insignia worn on khaki collar with branch-colour piping.)

M1939, Warrant officers *(Stražmistri). Štábní stražmistr, Vrchní stražmistr, Stražmistr:* 3–1 silver 5-point stars on branch-colour 4-sided collar patches. (**M1940,** no collar patches; insignia worn on khaki collar with branch-colour piping.)

M1939, Non-commissioned officers *(Poddůstojníci).*
Rotny: 3 white bone 5-point stars and 1 silver stud on branch-colour 4-sided collar patches. *Četar, Desátník:* 3–2 white bone 5-point stars on same collar patches. (**M1940,** no collar patches; insignia worn on khaki collar with branch-colour piping.)

M1939, Men *(Mužstvo). Svobodník, Vojin:* 1–0 white bone 5-point stars on same collar patches. (**M1940,** no collar patches; insignia worn on khaki collar with branch-colour piping.)

Operations

The Government Army's duties were guarding strategic rail lines and supporting civil defence units. In fact, the Germans did not trust the army, which was strongly anti-German, and many soldiers were dismissed for political unreliability. The 1st Bn guarded Protectorate President Emil Hácha in Prague Castle from November 1939. The 12 bands performed frequently in public, earning the Army the nickname of 'Hácha's Melody Boys'. The Government Army remained in the Protectorate from 1939 until May 1944, and was deployed during winter 1943/44 (with minimal success) to resist Czechoslovak Army parachutists from the Special Operations Executive in Great Britain (see below, "The SOE and Operation 'Anthropoid'").

Finally, on 8 May 1944, while 1st Bn remained in Prague, the 2nd–12th Bns were deployed to Mussolini's Italian Social Republic (RSI) in northern Italy to help guard transport links and vulnerable locations from increasing attacks by Italian partisans.[3] The units were assigned to 'Mobilized Inspectorates' as follows: *Zasazeny generálini inspektorát,* and *Zasazeny ínspektorát II* (Bologna): 6, 9 & 11 Bns (Chiari, later Verona); *Zasazeny ínspektorát I* (Varese): 2–5 Bns; *Zasazeny ínspektorát III* (Turin): 7, 8, 10 & 12 Battalions.

Of 4,958 men deployed to Italy, about 33 died in action against partisans or the Germans; and 1,403 deserted to the partisans, of whom 595 men escaped to Switzerland before joining the Czechoslovak Indep Armd Bde outside Dunkirk in August 1944. The remaining troops in Italy were disarmed on 4 October 1944, and reorganized into a Labour Bde to repair fortifications. In April 1945, the Bde mutinied and joined US Army forces, forming the '1st Czechoslovak Brigade in Italy'. Shortly afterwards they returned to Czechoslovakia, and helped Czechoslovak internal forces complete the liberation of Prague on 11 May 1945.

Resistance organizations

A number of organizations, drawn from various social groups, were formed in 1939 for resistance activities, such as factory sabotage and anti-German public demonstrations. The most important were the ON, PWZ and PU.

3   See also Elite 207, *World War II Partisan Warfare in Italy.*

The 'Defence of the Nation' *(Obrany národa* – ON) was the most effective organization created by former Czechoslovak Army personnel in April 1939. Commanded by retired Gen Josef Bílý, it was organized into Bohemia, Moravia, Prague and Greater Prague Regions (sing: *Zemské vojenské velitelstvo* – ZVV), and subdivided into 20 named Districts (sing: *Krajské Zemské vojenské velitelstvo* – KVV). The ON functioned until 11 May 1945, despite severe losses at the hands of the German security forces.

The 'Committee of the Petition We shall remain faithful' [i.e. to President Masaryk] *(Petiční vybor Věni zustaneme* – PWZ) recruited among the educated classes and trade unionists. Organized from August 1939, it provided Czech Military Intelligence in London, under Col František Moravec, with information on German operations. In autumn 1941, the PWZ suffered crippling losses from Gestapo raids, and in June 1942 it was liquidated.

The 'Political Centre' *(Politické ustredi* – PU) was formed in summer 1939 from pre-war Czechoslovak political parties (excluding the Communist Party). It concentrated on maintaining intelligence contacts with the Western Allies using a network of couriers, but was practically destroyed by German raids in spring 1940, leaving only a few individual activists.

In January 1940, these three organizations had formed the 'Central Leadership of Home Resistance' *(Ústredni vedeni odboje domácíciho* – ÚVOD) to coordinate their activities. Such activities decreased drastically as German repression increased, but civil disobedience culminating in a boycott on 14–21 September 1941 proved so successful that Hitler posted SS LtGen Reinhard Heydrich to Prague to crush Czechoslovak resistance permanently. Repression increased still further following Heydrich's assassination in June 1942, and by February 1943 ÚVOD activity was minimal.

Rotmistr (Warrant Officer Class 3) Jan Kubiš, one of the principal participants in the SOE's Operation 'Anthropoid' in May 1942 (compare with Plate D1). He wears the M1940 British-style officers' khaki service uniform, including the SD cap with WO's silver badge with crossed swords, and brown chin-strap. The open-collar SD tunic has cherry-red Infantry piping and two silver 5-point rank stars on the shoulder straps. Kubiš displays the ribbon of the 1939 War Cross, and another photo shows British Army parachutist's 'wings' on his upper right sleeve. Neither photo shows the M1940 red-lettered and edged 'CZECHOSLOVAKIA' national titles. (Photographer unknown; Wikimedia Commons/Public domain)

The SOE and Operation 'Anthropoid'

The Special Operations Executive (SOE) was formed on 22 July 1940 as a secret organization under the British Ministry of Economic Warfare. Its task to collect intelligence and support irregular and resistance warfare, mainly in states under enemy occupation.[4] Czechoslovaks, mostly members of the Czechoslovak Armed Forces in Great Britain, provided SOE with about 300 volunteers – a considerable achievement, given their restricted numbers. They were trained to be dropped into Bohemia–Moravia by parachute in teams of two or three, for intelligence-gathering and guerrilla activities in liaison with the resistance. There were about 97 such operations, each identified by a random name, starting with Operation 'Benjamin' on 16 April 1941 and ending with Operation 'Varjag' on 2 May 1945. Most of these operations have lapsed into obscurity, but Operation 'Anthropoid' – the assassination of Heydrich – is widely remembered.

Reinhard Heydrich, Himmler's intelligent and ruthless deputy at the Reich Security Headquarters (RSHA), was appointed Acting Governor of Bohemia–Moravia on 27 September 1941, and immediately built on his reputation, adding 'the Butcher of Prague' to his several nicknames. Meanwhile, Col Moravec of Czechoslovak Intelligence in London was under pressure to organize successful operations comparable to some

---

Independently of the London government-in-exile, the Soviet forces organized and supported communist partisans in the Protectorate. *Poručík* Ján Ušiak commanded the largest of these units, the 1st Czechoslovak 'Jan Žižka' Partisan Brigade. It was formed by Red Army-trained parachutists from 25 Aug 1944 and operational from Dec 1944, carrying out guerrilla warfare, sabotage and intelligence-gathering until it disbanded on 26 May 1945. Ušiak is wearing a Czechoslovak Army M1930 khaki field cap with a gilt metal Bohemian Lion and Shield badge, and an M1940 open-collared tunic with shirt and tie. (Prague liberation, 1945/Wikimedia Commons/Public domain)

achieved by other Allies. On 28 October 1941, two warrant officers, Jan Kubiš and Josef Gabčik, began training for 'Anthropoid', and on 28 December, they parachuted into Bohemia–Moravia, linking up with 2nd Lt Josef Valčík of the simultaneous Operation 'Silver A'.

Heydrich was careless in his movements around Prague, and on 27 May 1942 Kubiš, Gabčik and Valčík ambushed his open-topped Mercedes staff car. Severely wounded by debris from a grenade explosion, Heydrich died of sepsis on 4 June. The three-man team, now joined by four more parachutists, hid out in the crypt below the Sts Cyril and Methodius Orthodox church in Prague, but were betrayed for a reward of 1 million marks by the parachutist Karel Čurda, from Operation 'Outdistance'. German security troops surrounded the church, and at the culmination of a fierce gun battle they flooded the crypt; on 18 June 1942, the remaining parachutists shot themselves to avoid the risk of revealing information under torture.

Among the widespread repression that followed, a particularly shocking reprisal was the massacre and destruction on 10 June, by SS troops supported by Police and Reich Labour Service (RAD) personnel, of the villages of Lidice and Ležák. Among the villagers were relatives of the SOE 'Anthropoid' and 'Silver A' teams, and of the Czechoslovak forces in Great Britain. In total, some 5,000 people were killed and 13,000 more imprisoned as the SS tried to eliminate the intelligentsia of Bohemia–Moravia. The reprisals were so extreme that the Allies henceforth considered assassinations counter-productive, and during 1942–45 no other high-ranking Nazi was assassinated by SOE agents in Europe.

Continuing resistance

Since early 1942, both communists supported by the Soviet forces and non-communists supported by the London government-in-exile formed guerrilla groups in Bohemia–Moravia's urban areas – the first being the 'Green Cadre' *(Zeleny kádr)*. By 1944, about 50 groups had been formed, the most famous being the communist 1st Czechoslovak 'Jan Žižka' Partisan Bde, named after the famous medieval Czech military leader. Urban groups carried out sabotage missions, but German skill at penetrating these networks led to high losses. The coordinating ÚVOD was followed by the National Revolutionary Preparatory Commitee (PRNV) in June 1944, and 'the Council of Three' *(Rada Trī)* was also created that summer by ON and PWZ members, but disbanded in December 1944. By early 1945, communist partisans were dominant in the east of the Protectorate.

The battle for Prague

By January 1945, the Red Army's Czechoslovak corps, as part of 4th Ukrainian Front, had reached the Protectorate's eastern border. From February, despite their mutual suspicions, the internal communist and non-communist resistance groups formed a fragile alliance under a Czech National Committee *(Československá národní rada – ČNR)* to coordinate activities during a planned uprising to liberate Prague, the ČNR military

DÁMSKÉ KLOBOUKY Šamač

commander being Capt Jaromír Nechanský. The ON of former soldiers (under retired Gen František Slunéčko) remained a significant force, and on 30 April 1945 Gen Karel Kutlvašr was appointed commander of its Bartoš Force (city centre) while Gen Slunéčko would command in the suburbs. While initial insurgent strength would be only some 10,000, about half of them with firearms, support was promised by the armed Protectorate State Police and Gendarmerie, and by six Czech battalions of the German Air Raid Police (Luftschutzpolizei).

Among the occupiers, SS LtGen Karl Hermann Frank was overall commander, while LtGen Rudolf Toussaint headed German Army units in Prague, and SS MajGen Karl Friedrich von Pückler-Burghaus the Waffen-SS forces. The Allied powers had agreed on the division of territory liberated from the east and west, which would limit the ambitions of Gen George S. Patton and his US Third Army. On 1 May 1945, Marshal Ivan Konev's 1st Ukrainian Front began its advance on Prague, followed by Marshal Rodion Malinovsky's 2nd Ukrainian Front, and Marshal Andrey Yeryomenko's 4th Ukrainian Front including the Czechoslovak Army Corps.

Prague residents building a barricade across a street on 6 May 1945 during the uprising in the capital. They are among an estimated 30,000 insurgents who eventually fought in the battle for Prague, mostly without displaying any signs of party affiliations. (Vozka, Jaroslav/Wikimedia Commons/CC 4.0)

Prague crowds greet Marshal
of the Soviet Union Ivan Konev
(right, wearing greatcoat) on his
arrival in the city on 9 May 1945
at the head of the 1st Ukrainian
Front. Konev was the first
Allied commander to reach the
liberated capital. He and his staff
are wearing Red Army M1943
uniforms and insignia. (Karel
Hájek/Wikimedia Commons/
CC3.0)

In Prague, while armed uprisings by both communist and non-communist insurgents were planned for 7 May, inflammatory radio broadcasts on the 5th (and possibly news that Gen Patton's V Corps had reached Plzeň from the west on 4 May) led to scattered attacks on German troops and local collaborators. Fighting spread rapidly as Germans fired on the crowds, and Protectorate police fired back. By the night of the 5th, insurgents held most ground east of the Vltava River, including radio stations and the telephone exchange. They had liberated some 3,000 prisoners from the main jail, and had captured German weapons including Panzerfausts and even a few Hetzer armoured tank-destroyers.

Major-General Sergei Bunyachenko of the nearby German-formed Russian Liberation Army (ROA/KONR) then changed sides, and at noon on 6 May arrived with units of his 1st KONR Div from Beroun to fight beside the insurgents. The KONR seemed to tip the balance on 6–7 May, capturing the main rail station from Waffen-SS troops, but on the 8th they retreated in search of the illusory safety of surrender to the US Army. Intense Waffen-SS counterattacks on the 8th retook much of the lost ground as the insurgents began running out of ammunition. The street-fighting was savage, with many Czech prisoners and civilians killed out of hand, air raids (including by a couple of Me 262 jets of KG 51 on the radio station), and artillery fire.

Command decisions on both sides depended not only on the see-saw nature of the street-fighting, but also on the haphazard arrival of reports from elsewhere. On 5 May, GenFM Schörner of Army Group Centre had released troops including Waffen-SS armour to reinforce the Prague garrison; meanwhile, in the city, SS LtGen Frank was initiating the first contact with the ČNR. On the 6th, the arrival of the KONR division seemed to change the balance, but their withdrawal on the 8th encouraged the SS. On the 7th, GenFM Jodl had signed the unconditional surrender of German forces at Gen Eisenhower's SHAEF in Rheims, France, to take effect at one minute past midnight on 8/9 May. On 8 May, LtGen Toussaint and the ČNR negotiated the unhindered retreat westwards from Prague of all German troops, although some SS units were then still fighting stubbornly. The last of them had still not pulled out when, early on 9 May, the first Soviet tanks reached the suburbs.

After May 1945, Czechoslovak military and resistance forces were demobilized, and the pre-Munich borders were reconstituted. However, on 25 February 1948, the Czechoslovak Communist Party organized a *coup d'état* which installed a Soviet-controlled regime. Soldiers and airmen who had fought with the Western Allies were dismissed from service and often imprisoned, their reputations only to be rehabilitated officially after 29 March 1990, and the birth of the Democratic Czech and Slovak Federal Republic. (General Sergěj Ingr, a democracy activist, had died in 1956 – ostensibly of heart failure.)

SELECT BIBLIOGRAPHY

Kliment, Charles K. & Francev, Vladimír, *Czechoslovak Armored Fighting Vehicles 1918–1948* (Schiffer; Atglen, 1997)
Speychal, Robert, *Stráž obrany státu* (Prague, 2002)
Sluka, Jiri Fidler, *Encyklopedie branne moc 1920–1938* (Prague, 2006)
Vogeltanz, Jan, PhD & Polak, Milan; *Československe legie 1914–1918* (Paseda; Prague, 1998)
– *Československa Armáda 1918–1939* (Paseda; Prague, 1998)
Vogeltanz, Jan, PhD, Polak, Milan, & Hus, Miroslav, PhD, *Československa Armáda 1918–v zahraničí 1939–1945* (Paseda; Prague, 1998)
– *Vládní vojsko protektoratu Čechy a Morava 1939–1945* (Paseda; Prague, 2001)
– *Slovenská Armáda 1939–1945* (Paseda; Prague, 2001)
– *Československa Armáda 1945–1992* (Paseda; Prague, 2001)

PLATE COMMENTARIES

A: INTERNAL SECURITY, 1938–39

A1: *Armádni general* Jan Syrový; Prague, November 1938

Syrový had lost his right eye fighting in the Czechoslovak Legion under the Imperial Russian Army at the battle of Zborov (now Zboriv, Ukraine), 1–2 July 1917, and by 1918 he was commanding the Legion. He served as Army Chief of Staff (1 Jan 1926–11 Nov 1933); Inspector–General (12 Nov 1933–23 Sept 1938); Defence Minister (23 Sept 1938–27 Apr 1939); and Prime Minister (24 Sept 1938–1 Dec 1938), being obliged to sign the Munich Agreement on 30 Sept 1938. He retired on 27 Apr 1939, and was not active in the wartime resistance. On 14 May 1945, he was charged with collaboration and imprisoned, but was amnestied in 1960, and died in October 1970.

Syrový wears the M1930 service uniform of a Combat Arms general officer, with gilt crossed 'combat' swords on the gilt metal diamond-shaped badge of the peaked service cap. This also has gold twisted double chin-cords, gold lime-leaf edging to the peak, and red piping to the upper and lower edges of the band. His general officer's M1930 tunic has gilt metal buttons with the crossed-swords motif; 5-sided red collar patches with triple-leaf gold wire lime-branch embroidery; khaki shoulder straps with gold triple lime-leaf embroidery, gold braid inner edging and red outer piping; and four 5-point M1927 gold wire rank stars above the cuffs. He displays the silver General Staff graduation badge on his right breast pocket. His general officers' breeches have red seam piping between two red stripes.

A2: *Četar délesloužící*, 3rd Infantry Regiment 'Jan Žižka z Trocnova'

The 3rd Inf Regt's honour-title was the name of a medieval Bohemian general who defeated the German Teutonic Order at Grunwald (Grünfelde, East Germany) on 15 July 1410. This re-enlisted NCO commanding a section *(družstvo)* wears the M1930 khaki field uniform with a double-breasted greatcoat with two rows of 6 bronze buttons, khaki puttees and brown

Major-General Bohumil Miroslav (formerly Berdich Neumann) took command of the Czechoslovak Mixed Bde in Britain on 15 Aug 1940, was promoted lieutenant-general in 1943, and appointed Chief of General Staff in Sept 1944. He is wearing the khaki M1940 service tunic with gold lime-branch embroidery on red collar patches. His khaki shoulder straps have red piping outside gold inner edging, and M1943 rank insignia comprising a gilt star and crossed sword and scabbard. (Vozka, Jaroslav/Wikimedia Commons/Public domain)

ankle boots. The M1930 deep-flap peakless field cap (sidecap) has a re-enlisted NCO's silver Bohemian Lion and Shield badge on the left front, ahead of 3 silver rank studs. The three-point scalloped collar patches are in Infantry cherry-red; the khaki shoulder straps have cherry-red piping, 're-enlistment' centre-stripes, and base tabs bearing 3 silver rank studs. He wears his NCOs' silver 3rd Inf Regt badge on both sides of the collar in line with the shoulder straps. The red cloth lightning-bolt 'skills' badge on his left upper sleeve identifies him as a qualified telegraphist of a regimental signals platoon. He wears a brown leather belt and supporting straps, with a brass buckle-plate bearing the Bohemian Lion and Shield; two sets of paired ammunition pouches for his 7.92mm ČZ Vz.24 Mauser rifle; and a frogged bayonet scabbard. A canvas 'breadbag' haversack and an M1935 gas mask are slung over his right shoulder to his left hip.

A3: *Strážmistr,* Liberec Battalion, State Defence Guard, September 1938
This Police warrant officer assigned to the SOS wears an M1930 Czechoslovak State Police uniform with an Army M1932 helmet painted khaki. His black double-breasted greatcoat has two rows of 6 silver buttons embossed with a

Bohemian Lion and Shield, and red piping along the front edge (sometimes also seen on the cuffs and the rectangular flaps of the waist pockets). Rank insignia comprise silver rosettes and edging on bright red pointed collar patches for the lowest grade; gold rosettes and gold lime-leaf edging distinguished the highest grade. The policeman also wears a black M1930 tunic, breeches and riding boots. His equipment comprises a brown leather belt with a white-metal 2-claw buckle; two sets of double ammunition pouches, and the bayonet for his Vz.24 ifle.

B: CZECHOSLOVAK FORCES IN FRANCE, 1939–40
B1: *Kapitán* Alois Vašátko, I/5 Fighter Wing; Chartres, May 1940
Vašátko joined the French Armée de l'Air on 11 September 1939, and on 5 May 1940 was posted to Groupe de Chasse I/5 near Chartres, flying American Curtiss H75C-1 fighters. By 15 June, he was Czechoslovakia's top fighter ace in France and the fifth ace in the French Air Force, with 12 solo 'kills' and 3 shared.

Czechoslovak personnel wore French Armée de l'Air M1934 dark blue *('bleu Louise')* uniforms with Czechoslovak insignia. Vašátko wears a French sidecap with a gold Bohemian Lion and Shield and four 5-point gilt metal rank stars, the stars being repeated along the plain shoulder straps. On his right breast he displays the French M1916 pilot's qualification badge, comprising a gold star and wings on a silver oak-wreath, and on his left an M1923 Czechoslovak pilot's badge, of a silver sword and lime-wreath with a gold hilt, lion and wings. An unidentified triangular gold insignia is worn high on his left breast, above the ribbon of the 1939 Czech War Cross (narrow alternating vertical stripes in red (x6), white (x10), blue (x5), repeating red/white/blue/white/red/white, etc.

B2: *Štábní kapitán,* 1st Artillery Regiment, 1st Czechoslovak Division; Orléans, June 1940
Most officers of the 1st Czechoslovak Div wore the M1930 uniform with Czechoslovak rank insignia, omitting branch-colour collar patches and all insignia except rank (decorations were worn when appropriate).

This battery commander wears the British-style khaki M1930 service dress. The cap shows Artillery scarlet branch-colour band piping, a single gold plaited chin-cord, and the officers' gilt badge with 'combat' swords, but without the pre-1939 rank insignia on either side of the band. He has an open-collar tunic with box-pleated breast pockets with scalloped flaps and 'bellows' waist pockets, and his rank star on red-piped shoulder straps; breeches, and dark brown leather riding boots. Ranks below general officer could alternatively wear an M1939 French-style sidecap with rank insignia on the left side: gilt Bohemian Lion and Shield badge, 4–1 x 5-point stars above a gold bar (field officers); gilt Lion and Shield with 4–1 stars (subaltern officers); silver Lion and Shield with 4–2 stars (WOs); and bronze Lion and Shield with 4–0 silver studs (NCOs and men).

B3: *Vojín,* 2nd Infantry Regiment, 1st Czechoslovak Division
This infantry private wears a French M1926 helmet without a frontal plate, and basic French Army M1935 khaki field uniform as introduced 10 January 1936. This comprises an M1920/35 tunic with 6 khaki-painted front buttons, red-piped shoulder straps, no collar insignia or breast pockets, and two internal waist pockets with diagonal external flaps without buttons, worn with M1938 trousers, khaki cloth puttees and